Women Are Kingmakers!

CELEBRATING GOD'S GREAT IDEA: WOMEN!

WELLINGTON BOONE

Atlanta, Georgia

Women Are Kingmakers

© 2012 Wellington Boone

http://wellingtonboone.com
http://www.kingmakers.org
http://shop.apptepublishing.com
Phone: 404-840-8443

APPTE Publishing
5875 Peachtree Industrial Blvd Ste 300
Norcross, Georgia 30092

The following abbreviations are used to identify versions of the Bible used in this book:

AMP Amplified Bible. Scripture quotations taken from the Amplified® Bible, Copyright © 1954, 1958, 1962, 1964, 1965, 1987 by The Lockman Foundation Used by permission. (www.Lockman.org)

KJV *King James Version,* also known as the *Authorized Version.* (Public domain)

The Message Scripture quotations from THE MESSAGE. Copyright © by Eugene H. Peterson 1993, 1994, 1995, 1996, 2000, 2001, 2002. Used by permission of NavPress Publishing Group.

NASB Scripture quotations taken from the New American Standard Bible®, Copyright © 1960, 1962, 1963, 1968, 1971, 1972, 1973, 1975, 1977, 1995 by The Lockman Foundation Used by permission. (www.Lockman.org)

NIV The Holy Bible, New International Version®, NIV® Copyright © 1973, 1978, 1984, 2011 by Biblica, Inc.™ Used by permission. All rights reserved worldwide.

NKJV Scripture taken from the New King James Version®. Copyright © 1982 by Thomas Nelson, Inc. Used by permission. All rights reserved.

NLT Scripture quotations marked NLT are taken from the Holy Bible, New Living Translation, copyright © 1996, 2004, 2007 by Tyndale House Foundation. Used by permission of Tyndale House Publishers, Inc., Carol Stream, Illinois 60188. All rights reserved. New Living, NLT, and the New Living Translation logo are registered trademarks of Tyndale House Publishers.

TLB The Living Bible, Copyright © 1971. Used by permission of Tyndale House Publishers, Inc., Carol Stream, Illinois 60188. All rights reserved.

Nouns and pronouns referring to deity are capitalized throughout the text of this book unless they are included within a direct quotation, in which case the original capitalization is retained.
Includes bibliographical references

ISBN: 0-9847821-6-8
ISBN 13: 978-0-9847821-6-1

Printed in the United States of America. Third Edition October 2012

Contents

More Books by Bishop Wellington Boone

Breaking Through: Taking the Kingdom into the Culture by Out-Serving Others (Nashville: Broadman and Holman, 1996). ISBN 0-8054-5396-2.

Dare to Hope: A 30-Day Journey to Hope (Atlanta: APPTE Publishing, 2009). ISBN: 978-0-9776892-8-6.

Holy Ghost Is My Friend: A Great Friend Who Must Never Be Ignored Again (Atlanta: APPTE Publishing, 2011). ISBN: 9780984782109.

Low Road To New Heights: What it Takes to Live Like Christ in the Here and Now (New York, NY: Doubleday, 2002). ISBN: 0-385-50087-4.

My Journey with God (Atlanta: APPTE Publishing, coming in 2012). ISBN-13 978-0-9776892-6-2. ISBN 10: 0-9776892-6-3.

Your Wife Is Not Your Momma: How You Can Have Heaven In Your Home. (Atlanta: APPTE Publishing, 2011). ISBN: 978-0-9776892-9-3.

Bishop Boone's resources are available online at www.wellingtonboone.com, http://www.Amazon.com, and http://shop.apptepublishing.com

Additional resources are available on pages 232-234.

Wellington Boone Ministries
5875 Peachtree Industrial Blvd Ste 300
Norcross, GA 30092

Phone: 404-840-8443
APPTEPublishing@Gmail.com

Introduction

"Thou excellest them all."[1]

In every area of society, some women stand out from the crowd. I call them Kingmakers. They're the women that people remember. They're the women that people should listen to. They're the wives, mothers, teachers, and managers who helped others become what they are today. You don't see the mom behind a person who becomes great, but she's a Kingmaker, whether you see her or not. She's under acknowledged and underappreciated, but she's a Kingmaker just the same.

A Kingmaker is the wife that every man wants. She's the woman you want to manage your company. She's the team player who helps you to win.

For a Kingmaker, no task is too difficult; no sacrifice too great. She's got an inner substance of life that makes a difference in the lives of others. She's a Kingmaker.

A Kingmaker has the power of influence over another person's life and the ability from God to make that person great.

Are you a Kingmaker?

When you meet a Kingmaker, it doesn't take long to realize she's authentic. She's the real thing. You just love her integrity and her lack of manipulation. You see a woman without guile. A woman who doesn't try to build her self-esteem at your expense. She's already received her sense of value from Jesus. She's fulfilled. She knows God loves her, and that's where she gets her self-worth.

When people fail her and fall short in their relationships with her, she doesn't reject them. She draws on her inner strength to keep loving them, because she's grateful that God didn't reject her.

You can be that kind of woman.

---

[1] Proverbs 31:29 KJV.

Proverbs speaks of wives like that as the wives who excel them all.[2] Hebrews 11 says that "God is not ashamed to be called their God: for he hath prepared for them a city." [3]

When you're a Kingmaker, nobody has to praise you all the time to keep you going, because you live in anticipation of the praise you'll get in Heaven. To you, that's better than getting rewards now. You don't live just for today. You live with the end in view—the next life. You know you have a future—God's future. You're purifying yourself and becoming Christ-like daily in every thought, word, and deed. When you see Him, you'll be like Him. You're growing more like Him every day.

| *You're becoming like Jesus* | *". . . but we know that, when he shall appear, we shall be like him; for we shall see him as he is."[4]* |

God Values Women!
Women are undervalued by the culture, but not by God. The same One who gave man his purpose and value also gave it to woman. He said she's a help capable for him.

> *A woman has the ability to add something to everyone she comes in contact with. I call her a Kingmaker because she makes others into something great—a great husband or daughter or whoever they are.*

There's something God gave her that adds to what the man is. A Kingmaker is a lifter. She carries people from her position of humility—her position of lowliness. She doesn't carry people from above them but she carries them from beneath. She's like Christ! There isn't anything in the Kingdom of God that doesn't relate to lifting. Even when you're in a high position, you're lifting others below you.

---

[2] See Proverbs 31:29.
[3] Hebrews 11:16 KJV.
[4] 1 John 3:2 KJV.

That's something Jesus does, and I want to honor those who are like Jesus.

A few years ago, I released a series of three audio messages called "Women Who Are Kingmakers" that described Kingmaker Wives who sacrificially help their husbands fulfill their God-given potential—women like my wife Katheryn. If you had known me when I first married her, and then compared that man to the man I've become now, you would understand that these Kingmaker principles really work. I'm a living example of someone whose life was changed by a Kingmaker.

> *Kingmaking is not just for women. It's a Kingdom principle that applies to men as well as women. True Kingmaking transcends gender. It takes you beyond gender and into the relationship of Christ and the Church. However, women seem to understand this principle better than men, so I'm dedicating this book to women who are Kingmakers.*

The album "Women Who Are Kingmakers" quickly became my best-selling series, and I began to receive requests from women wanting a book on that subject. As I continued to explore this topic, it became clear to me that Kingmaking applies to more areas of a woman's life than just marriage. I began to see it as a generational call to women to change the world! I made a commitment to produce a spiritual and practical book to show women that they have a calling on their lives to be Kingmakers.

Kingmakers are people who are like Jesus. They are willing to humble themselves to help someone else fulfill his or her destiny. In reality, that is the call of every Christian.

FEARLESS FEMALE: CLARA BARTON

During the Civil War, a single woman named Clara Barton stepped onto the battlefield and became a Kingmaker to the wounded soldiers. In the night, she prayed for the dying soldiers' wives and sisters, and she prayed for herself, so overwhelmed with their plight. Wartime field nursing was something women had never done. At first she was not welcomed by the commanders, but she was so respectful and helpful that soon their resentment was replaced with gratitude because she brought her own bandages, and lanterns to light the night. In later years she founded the American Red Cross, and created an agency to identify the dead and notify their families. She never married but dedicated her life to serving others. She was a Kingmaker. She wrote to her cousin about being a Christian woman on the front lines, serving others sacrificially:

Kingmakers
In History

Clara Barton
(1821-1912)

Founder of American Red Cross is moved with compassion as she considers the grief that will come to the soldiers' loved ones when they die.

"Oh northern mothers, wives and sisters, all unconscious of the hour, would to Heaven that I could bear for you the concentrated woe which is so soon to follow, would that Christ would teach my soul a prayer that would plead to the Father for grace sufficient for you, God pity and strengthen you every one."

THE WOMEN WHO WENT TO THE FIELD
By Clara Barton

"And these were the women who went to the war:
The women of question; what did they go for?
Because in their hearts God had planted the seed
Of pity for woe, and help for its need;
They saw, in high purpose, a duty to do,
And the armor of right broke the barriers through. . . .
And the man liveth not who could say to them nay;
They would stand with you now, as they stood with you then,
The nurses, consolers, and saviours of men."

MARRIAGE AND THE RELATIONSHIP
BETWEEN CHRIST AND THE CHURCH

Clara Barton never married, but marriage demonstrates something else about Kingmaking's spiritual significance—the relationship of Christ and the Church. When my wife and I got married, we had never heard that marriage demonstrated something about the reality of the Kingdom of God. We didn't understand the meaning of the biblical role of a husband as representing Jesus and a wife as representing His Bride, the Church. People stayed married "for the sake of the children" in those days, but we didn't understand that it's even more important to *stay married for the sake of Jesus.* Married for the sake of Jesus? That's really getting back to the basics.

The cause of Christ is advanced when a wife is a Kingmaker submitted to her husband in the same way as it is advanced when the Church submits to Christ. It is advanced when a husband willingly gives his life for his wife, showing the sacrifice of Jesus for the Church.

The Christ-like character of a husband and wife in marrying and staying married looks good to God, and it looks good to the people around you, too. With divorce statistics staying the way they are, a good marriage should be the talk of the town. It should make the evening news on all the networks. More and more people are marrying and staying married, because of Christ.

People will be blessed by your commitment	*"People everywhere keep telling me about your lives of faith, and every time I hear them, I thank him."*[5]

On their wedding day, a man and woman create something new—both spiritually and naturally—that can be seen and read of men. Their faithfulness to keep their covenant in later years speaks of the eternal bond between Jesus and the Church. As years pass, their relationship brings the Kingdom of God into reality before the eyes of the world, as they carry the will of God in the womb of their spirit. People can see that this Kingdom is reality! It's real!

In earlier times, marriage vows like the ones in the Book of Common Prayer emphasized the lifetime covenant of a husband and wife. They read, "For richer, for poorer, till death us do part." When a woman commits herself to her husband on earth it's a death covenant. It's a covenant as serious as committing to almighty God for saving grace. If either spouse breaks the covenant of marriage, how can he or she be trusted with anything else? The covenant-keeping commitment of a Kingmaker—in marriage, ministry, or the marketplace—is a building block of integrity and Christ-likeness.

Kingmakers forsake all others, just as Jesus did Marriage Ceremony *from* The Book of Common Prayer *(1662)*[6]	"The Minister shall say, *Wilt thou have this man to thy wedded husband, to live together after God's ordinance in the holy estate of Matrimony? Wilt thou obey him, and serve him, love, honour, and keep him in sickness and in health; and, forsaking all other, keep thee only unto him, so long as ye both shall live?* "The Woman shall answer, *I will.*"

---

[5] Romans 1:8 *The Message*.
[6] "The Form of Solemnization of Matrimony" From *The Book of Common Prayer* (1662 Version) online at http://www.weddings.co.uk/info/wedserv.htm. Accessed July 2012.

When I was growing up, I never had an example of a happy marriage and family, but out of my relationship with God I discovered spiritual truths about marriage that have made our marriage last. Women can learn to be Kingmakers, regardless of their past. Whether you are married or not, whether you've had a good life or a tough one, *you can learn to live the way God wants.* You just have to know Him and learn His ways.

Becoming the Best

I used to crop tobacco when I was a kid, and I remember how much pride we put into it. I got paid a dollar an hour for cropping tobacco, and you better believe that I earned it! You can imagine what it was like bending over for hours in the hot sun, walking along the field, and as far as you could see, there was no end. You started early in the morning—practically before day—and you went around those stalks, grabbing that tobacco and holding it under your arms. It was wet and gooey, and it was so early in the morning that it was cold! When you got your arms full, you put it on the truck, and you ran back and started cropping some more.

Even though my back was bent over and I was tired and wet, I was determined to beat those other croppers. When I first began, all of them were better at the task and faster than I was. They not only knew how to go around that stalk, they also knew how to do it quickly. My back would be hurting, and by the time I'd stand up and stretch they were about another ten yards in front of me and the truck was gone. I had to run to keep up.

The reason that the other guys and I would race to the end of the field every day was that we took pride in wanting to be the best cropper. It wasn't just the dollar that we were after. It was the mentality of being somebody. If we were so reduced down that we had to be sharecroppers, we wanted to be the best sharecroppers there were!

It's the same principle when you're working for God. You want to be the best Kingmaker He has. Somebody might put you down for being a woman, but when you come to the end of your field and face Jesus on that Great Day, He can say to you, "You did a great job under incredibly difficult conditions. Well done!"

**Well
done!**

*"His lord said unto him, Well done, thou good
and faithful servant: thou hast been faithful over
a few things, I will make thee ruler over many
things: enter thou into the joy of thy lord."[7]*

This life is a race that you're competing in, and you run to
win. This field of life is more important than winning the Olympics
or the tennis championship of the world, because other people's lives
are at stake—the people whom your life touches. You run well *for
them*. Paul said there are many who run the race, but only one wins
the crown. He said, *"Run to win."*

**Run to win,
with purpose in
every step**

*"Remember that in a race everyone runs, but
only one person gets the prize. You also must
run in such a way that you will win. All athletes
practice strict self-control. They do it to win a
prize that will fade away, but we do it for an
eternal prize. So I run straight to the goal with
purpose in every step."[8]*

Live a life so full of grace and purpose that there's no doubt
that you resemble Christ. No one has a better attitude than you. No
one is a better servant. Greatness with God is not all about thinking
you're better than someone else and walking all over people. You're
a winner with God when you *help* people and serve them, as Jesus
did. You're great at loving, generous in giving, intense in dedication,
full of good works, and longsuffering. When people mistreat you,
you maintain an attitude like the Lord. Your selflessness amazes
others. You have all kinds of people around you whom you have
made great. You're a Kingmaker!

In the following chapters, I will show you some exciting
examples of women just like you who became Kingmakers in their
generation. Some were known by Presidents, some by slaves, and
others simply by their families. But you can be sure that everyone
who becomes a Kingmaker for Christ will be known in Heaven.

---

[7] Matthew 25:21 KJV.
[8] 1 Corinthians 9:24-26 NLT.

SECTION 1

Getting the
Mind of the King

Chapter 1
Starting and Finishing Well

"You've all been to the stadium and seen the athletes race.
Everyone runs; one wins. Run to win. All good athletes train
hard. They do it for a gold medal that tarnishes and fades.
You're after one that's gold eternally. I don't know about you,
but I'm running hard for the finish line.
I'm giving it everything I've got." [1]

Woman! You're a Kingmaker! The Lord doesn't have to look any further, because He has you. You're the one He can use to fulfill His purposes in the earth. Life is a race to fulfill the will of God, and you're a finisher!

You use your gifts and abilities to make others great. Your influence changes history. You don't care if you get credit in this world, because God will reward you in the next. You're a Kingmaker.

You're the first woman, formed and shaped by God to be a perfect helper to the man.

You're the Church, Christ's woman, "a bride adorned for her husband,"[2] making Jesus King.

You're a Kingmaker! This is the season for your significance. You've been hand-picked by God. You're special. There's nobody just like you.

God formed you and Jesus Christ is working inside of you by the Holy Ghost to take you to the next level of development in your spiritual life.

You're becoming so transformed that you see others around you who have not come up to your level, and you treat them like kings. You're a Kingmaker!

---

[1] 1 Corinthians 9:24-26, *The Message.*
[2] Revelation 21:2 KJV.

Running like Jesus, a finisher	*"Wherefore seeing we also are compassed about with so great a cloud of witnesses, let us lay aside every weight, and the sin which doth so easily beset us, and let us run with patience the race that is set before us, Looking unto Jesus the author and finisher of our faith; who for the joy that was set before him endured the cross, despising the shame, and is set down at the right hand of the throne of God."* [3]

GOD ISN'T FINISHED WITH YOU YET

I'm not always sensitive to my wife or truly sacrificial in my love, but that's because God isn't finished with me yet. The same is true of you. We're a work in progress! The great focus of God is finishing up His work *in us*. God is finishing up His work on the earth, and you are the earth that He is finishing. You came from the dust of the ground. You are earth dust that God is shaping.

Formed by the Lord for His purposes	*"And the LORD God formed man of the dust of the ground, and breathed into his nostrils the breath of life; and man became a living soul."* [4]

In your secret prayer closet with Jesus, He shapes you to become more like Him. You understand His will and learn to obey Him, even as you love Him. When Jesus said in Matthew 6, "Thy will be done in earth as it is in Heaven," the tendency would be for us to immediately focus on the physical planet Earth, but the will of God that interests Him is the will of God in *your* earth. He is putting *you* into shape. He is working *you* into His likeness, and then because of the beauty inside of you, you beautify everything else. Sometimes we forget what God is doing inside of us and we become focused on *what we are going through* rather than *how we are going through it*. We forget that the thing that God is doing *in us* is more

---

[3] Hebrews 12:1-2 KJV.
[4] Genesis 2:7 KJV.

important than what someone else is doing *to us*. That's character. Kingmaking goes beyond serving people and making them great. It includes the development of Christ-like character.

It is not meeting people's needs that makes you a Kingmaker, but *staying in the character of Christ as you meet their needs*. As you deal with relationships from a position of humility, you are becoming like Christ.

God Believes in You

One of the greatest encouragements you can have is that Jesus has confidence in you. He believes in you! He will not stop helping you to become a Kingmaker.

God will keep working on your strengths	*"There has never been the slightest doubt in my mind that the God who started this great work in you would keep at it and bring it to a flourishing finish on the very day Christ Jesus appears."*[5]

Are you a Kingmaker to a husband or child or manager who tries your patience and makes you wonder if you're cut out for this? Do you want to give up before you bring them out of their attitudes and into their kingship? Press on!

Almost all of us are functioning at a level of character that falls beneath our call, but God still uses us. He can use you. He can use that person who is driving you to your knees. Hang in there! That brother or sister needs you. Don't give up!

If God used only qualified people, we would all be in trouble, but He uses imperfect people. Because of that, you can be sure that He will get praise and honor in the end—yet still give you rewards! That's the awesome thing about being saved.

WOMEN IN THE PURPOSE OF GOD

In the redemptive work of God, a woman who can see herself

---

[5] Philippians 1, *The Message*.

as she is, beyond all her circumstances and the babble of the day, is someone who can make anyone great, even if they are not at the level where they should be. She never gives up on people, even if she is the only one left who believes in them.

Moving Past What You Need to What You Can Do

When you have an unlimited, eternal perspective instead of a limited, worldly perspective, you can get unstuck from the gender babble related to gender rights, because you have moved from a gender mentality into a kingdom mentality. Even if you're in a position of humility—let me go further, even a position of humiliation—in this world, you are in a high position from Heaven's view when you stop looking at *what you need* and instead look at *what you can do.*

Women have been taught for so long that the man is your covering, which he is. And that you're the weaker vessel, which you are. But if you look at your womanhood redemptively you will recognize that God has placed strength in you that He is calling you to use for His purposes in this hour.

Kingmakers in History

Wife of John Bunyan
(1625-1656)
Author of
Pilgrim's Progress

He gave glory to God for his godly wife and her family.

John Bunyan, who would later be imprisoned for his faith and write the classic Pilgrim's Progress, *was on a path of destruction until he married his wife. She was poor, but brought with her into the marriage her inheritance—two books that her Puritan father had left her:* The Plain Man's Pathway to Heaven, *and* The Practice of Piety. *Those books changed his life. He said, "My mercy was to light upon a wife whose father was counted godly."[6]*

---

[6] Rev. George Cheever, "A Memoir on John Bunyan" (Published in George Offor's 1861 edition of *Bunyan's Works*, 1861). Online at http://acacia.pair.com/Acacia.John.Bunyan/Sermons.Allegories/Memoir.On.John.Bunyan.html. Accessed July 2012.

Whether you have a husband or you are single, you have in you as a woman something that speaks about Who God is. In the creative work of God, He decided your gender before you were born. He will use it for His purposes!

Don't ever let anybody tell you that you are at a disadvantage as a female. God, before the foundation of the world, said you would be the woman you are. Your womanhood relates to the purposes of God and to the whole earth itself.

God gave the woman to Adam, and Adam was blessed, but he didn't take good care of her. Adam sat there in the Garden and kept his mouth shut while the devil was talking to his woman, and that caused the woman to have to fend for herself. Many men are keeping their mouths shut right now and letting their wives out-pray them. She is fighting off the devil over their children, and she is fighting off the devil over their house, and she is fighting off the devil over their finances, but he is just like Adam. Silent.

In my book *Your Wife Is Not Your Momma* I devoted an entire chapter to the subject "Women Should Marry Only Grown-Up Men." However, we men have to admit that even when we are grown up, we still need the help of our woman.

A Kingmaker has to function at another level. She's the greatest thing in the garden. God made her and brought her to the man. The Bible says when a man loves his wife he loves himself.[7] It's serious business to have a Kingmaker Woman.

Great Woman behind a Man

Behind every great man is a great woman. Behind Jesus being recognized as great in the earth is a great woman, the Church. Remember, a Kingmaker is someone with the power to influence another person's life and the ability from God to take that person into greatness.

Kingmaker women serve others so seriously that they take them some place they could never get to on their own. In the

---

[7] See Ephesians 5:28.

process, both of them become great, because Jesus said the greatest is the one who serves.

The greatest ***serves***	*"But he that is greatest among you shall be* *your servant."[8]*

A Kingmaker Woman might be—

- A wife
- A mother or grandmother
- An executive or secretary
- A teacher
- A missionary, nurse, or minister
- A sister or daughter

She has laid aside her self-interests and focused on others, just like Jesus. She is able to move beyond looking solely on her own things, and is able to look on the things of others.[9]

"If I then, your Lord and Master,
have washed your feet; ye also ought to wash one
another's feet. For I have given you an example,
that ye should do as I have done to you."[10]

JERUSHA EDWARDS: YOUNG, SINGLE, DEDICATED

Maybe you're single and want to be married so you ask, "What about me? I'm not married yet." *You're being trained for greatness whether you are married or not.* If God wants you to be married, there is some man out there whom you're going to make into a King. Right now you're maintaining yourself. You're walking in godliness. You're not defined by earthly distinctions. You have come from Heaven, and God says, "I'm going to use you in a mighty way."

---

[8] Matthew 23:11 KJV.
[9] See Philippians 2:4-5.
[10] John 13:14-15 KJV.

In the early days of our nation, the great theologian Jonathan Edwards took into his home a dying young missionary named David Brainerd who had given his life to save the Native Americans. Brainerd's influence extended past his lifetime because he kept a personal journal that he filled with anguished thoughts about his need to be more like Christ. After his death, Edwards published it. Years later, John Wesley, like many other great men of his day, read Brainerd's journal and urged others to read it, because of its life-changing words.

Brainerd's stay in the home of Jonathan Edwards was his last home on earth. Edwards' teenage daughter, Jerusha, who had been his devoted nurse, died also, four months later.

Edwards wrote of her death without bitterness, such was his confidence in God and in his Kingmaker daughter who had responded to God. This is what he said:

Kingmakers In History

Jerusha Edwards
(1729-1747)

Daughter of Jonathan Edwards, American Theologian

She ended her days caring for David Brainerd, dying at the age of 17.

Jonathan Edwards said she "was fitted to deny herself for God and to do good, beyond any young woman whatsoever that he knew of. She had manifested a heart uncommonly devoted to God in the course of her life, many years before her death; and said on her deathbed, that she had not seen one minute for several years, wherein she desired to live one minute longer, for the sake of any other good in life, but doing good, living to God, and doing what might be for His glory."[11]

---

[11] Jonathan Edwards, *Works of Jonathan Edwards*, Volume One, Chapter XV, "Arrival of David Brainerd at Northampton." Online at http://www.ccel.org/ccel/edwards/works1.i.xv.html. Accessed July 2012.

SARAH: KINGMAKER WIFE BEHIND ABRAHAM

Abraham is the father of faith, but like every great man, he had a woman behind him. He wasn't always at the level where he was called to be, but God gave him a Kingmaker wife.

In Genesis Chapter 12 and Chapter 20 are two stories that expose Abraham as someone who couldn't make it without a Kingmaker for a wife. Behind the great man, Abraham, was a great woman, Sarah. Twice in the Bible we see that Abraham, fearing for his life, denied being married to Sarah and allowed a king to take her into his harem. There could hardly be a greater betrayal, a greater abdication of the protective role of husband, than for a man to put his wife in danger of being violated by another man in order to protect himself. Can you imagine what it took for her to submit to Abraham under those circumstances? Can you imagine the emotional challenges that she was facing? It's amazing to think about the kind of inner strength it must have taken for her to reverence him and call him "Lord." Abraham became the "father of faith," but Sarah was the woman of faith[12] he needed. She was his Kingmaker.

Biblical Kingmakers	*"For in this manner, in former times, the holy women who trusted in God also adorned themselves, being submissive to their own husbands, as Sarah obeyed Abraham, calling him lord."*[13]
Sarah, Wife of Abraham *Woman of Faith, submitted to God and her husband*	

When Sarah submitted herself to her husband, despite her husband's inexcusable selfishness and cowardice, both times God Himself protected her. He plagued Pharaoh's household with many plagues (Genesis 12:17), visited Abimelech in a dream (Genesis 20:3-7), and cursed Abimelech's household with barrenness because of Sarah (Genesis 20:18). Both times that Abraham sent his wife off unprotected, these supernatural visitations caused Sarah to be released unharmed.

---

[12] Hebrews 11:11-12 NKJV.
[13] 1 Peter 3:5-6 NKJV.

Abraham, the patriarch whose lineage gave rise to the entire Jewish people and ultimately gave birth to Jesus, the Savior of the world, was supported by a true Kingmaker, a woman, in a time and culture with much greater gender restrictions than we know today. She had the power and faith to shape the course of history through her obedience to God.

You're a Kingmaker when you make a man something that without you he couldn't possibly become. Your thoughts for yourself and him are unlimited. You always believe that God is at work on your behalf and on his behalf.

If it wasn't for God coming against this king of Egypt and bringing His hammer down on him, Sarah would have been stuck in that harem. Both times God had to show up for her. This woman said, "I'm married to a patriarch, and even though he has shortcomings I'm going to maintain my position of voluntary subjection, because he can never be what he is ordained to be unless I can be what I'm ordained to be. I do not live just for the supply that I can get from my husband. I make him into a king, because I'm a Kingmaker myself. I come from the royal lineage. I don't look the way the rest of the world looks. I don't have the seductive appearance of worldly women. I don't have to dress up my hair to look sensual, and try to wear sexually explicit clothes and draw men to my body. I'm married, and I'm a Kingmaker."

A lot of women might say that Sarah's experience with Abraham's reckless disregard for her safety would justify divorce, but Kingmaking is one of those things that keeps people married. It's a divine empowerment from God that makes marriage work. Once a man and woman marry, that's it. There's no "wiggle room." You stand flat-footed. Except in the most extreme circumstances that Jesus defined, *divorce is not an option*. You decide in advance that you will marry and stay married, "till death us do part," and then you learn how.

| **God hates** | *"For the LORD God of Israel says* |
| **divorce** | *That He hates divorce."[14]* |

---

[14] Malachi 2:16 NKJV.

HOLY ESTATE OF MATRIMONY

Marriage is holy. It was instituted by God. The apostle Paul said, "Marriage is honorable among all."[15] Anyone who changes the definition of marriage should have the fear of God on them, because it was instituted by God in a specific way that cannot be changed. It is "Holy Matrimony."

The commitment of Adam to Mrs. Adam and the husband to his wife in their marriage vows is important not only for the success of a couple's marriage, but also as a picture of the relationship between Christ and His Bride, the Church. Marriage is not all about you. It's all about God and representing the Kingdom of God.

Marriage represents Christ and the Church	*"Therefore as the church is subject unto Christ, so let the wives be to their own husbands in every thing. Husbands, love your wives, even as Christ also loved the church, and gave himself for it."[16]*

Mrs. Adam was presented to Mr. Adam by God as the bride is presented to the groom by her father. The Bride of Christ is presented by God the Father to Jesus. The Church is such a Kingmaker to Jesus that when she is presented to Him, He knows she came from the Father. They have the same spirit, the same thoughts, words, and deeds. What He would say, the Church says also. What He would do, the Church does also.

---

[15] Hebrews 13:4 NKJV.
[16] Ephesians 5:24-25 KJV.

Marriage represents the eternal union between Christ and the Church

Wedding Ceremony from Book of Common Prayer (1662)[17]

"Dearly beloved, we are gathered together here in the sight of God, and in the face of this congregation, to join together this Man and this Woman in holy Matrimony; which is an honourable estate, instituted of God in the time of man's innocency, signifying unto us the mystical union that is betwixt Christ and his Church; which holy estate Christ adorned and beautified with his presence, and first miracle that he wrought, in Cana of Galilee; and is commended of Saint Paul to be honourable among all men: and therefore is not by any to be enterprised, nor taken in hand, unadvisedly, lightly, or wantonly, to satisfy men's carnal lusts and appetites, like brute beasts that have no understanding; but reverently, discreetly, advisedly, soberly, and in the fear of God; duly considering the causes for which Matrimony was ordained."

When the preacher asks the husband the following questions, he answers "Yes" with all his heart, because he knows he's marrying a Kingmaker.

Man's marriage commitment for life

Wedding Ceremony from Book of Common Prayer (1662)[18]

"Wilt thou have this woman to thy wedded wife, to live together after God's ordinance in the holy estate of Matrimony? Wilt thou love her, comfort her, honour, and keep her in sickness and in health; and, forsaking all other, keep thee only unto her, so long as ye both shall live?"

---

[17] "The Form of Solemnization of Matrimony" From *The Book of Common Prayer* (1662 Version) online at http://www.weddings.co.uk/info/wedserv.htm. Accessed July 2012.
[18] Ibid.

When the preacher asks the bride the following questions, she answers "Yes!" with all her heart:

Woman's marriage commitment for life *Wedding Ceremony from Book of Common Prayer (1662)* [19]	*"Wilt thou have this man to thy wedded husband, to live together after God's ordinance in the holy estate of Matrimony? Wilt thou obey him, and serve him, love, honour, and keep him in sickness and in health; and, forsaking all other, keep thee only unto him, so long as ye both shall live?"*

In God's view of marriage, the husband loves the wife and the wife loves the husband. When the husband blesses his wife, he blesses himself. "He that loveth his wife loveth himself."[20] When the wife loves her husband, she blesses herself.

KINGMAKER SINGLE MISSIONARY: JOANNA MOORE

Joanna Moore, a Baptist missionary after the Civil War, was a single Kingmaker Teacher sent from God to make kings of the black men who were pastors to the freed slaves. Although she was white, she did not look down on the humble black men trying to live a Christ-like lifestyle before their people. She was a Kingmaker.

Joanna Moore was a woman whom God used to take those pastors some place they couldn't get to on their own, just as the first woman did for the first man, Adam.

She was God's great idea.

Women are God's great idea.

Say this, *I am God's great idea!*

---

[19] Ibid.
[20] Ephesians 5:28 KJV.

Kingmakers
In History

Joanna P. Moore
(1832-1916)

*Teacher to former slaves
who became pastors*

"I helped Rev. George W. Walker in his Sabbath school. He was one of the most honorable, straightforward, reliable preachers we had then in New Orleans. A teacher of his Sunday school, who was a Christian, had died about a year before and left him without a Christian in his school, except a deacon who would come in and open with prayer. He told me that he would often rise at midnight to ask God to send a teacher for his Sabbath school, 'And now, Sister Moore,' he said, 'you are an answer to my prayer. Surely God did send you.'"[21]

Notice that there is no condescension in this message to new pastors, just instruction and encouragement from a Kingmaker:

"Dear pastors, the reason your converts backslide is because you starve them to death. What would you think of a parent who starved her child? Pastors often scold the members for doing wrong, but cross words do not feed. God's word must daily be eaten. You should prepare the word in small doses so that it can be taken in. The sincere milk of the word makes them grow strong, 1 Peter, 2:2. After the milk food, gradually give them stronger diet. You must plan some way to have them eat daily; one good meal on Sunday will not suffice. So I taught the pastors, and in my work at this time may be seen the working out of the conception that found its final expression in the Fireside School."[22]

---

[21] Joanna Moore, *In Christ's Stead* (Chicago: Women's Baptist Home Mission Society, 1902), p. 51. Available online at http://docsouth.unc.edu/church/moore/moore.html#jmoor41. Accessed July 2012.
[22] Ibid.

THE WOMAN—GOD'S GREAT IDEA

Mrs. Adam was God's great idea! He made the woman because the man wasn't good enough all by himself. God didn't say the man was *no good*, but implied he was *not good enough*. God saw a need in the man and filled it with a woman. He created her as a perfect mate, a partner in all that he would do. She was capable of every assignment. She was the missing element in his life. Here are some reasons why God created the woman, God's great idea.

1. Creating the woman as a helper for man was God's great idea. He saw that man needed some serious help to make it! For every man who becomes great, some awesome woman helped him get there. That's not the only assignment that God has for a woman, but it's a creative one.

Not good for a man to be alone	*"And the LORD God said, It is not good that the man should be alone; I will make him an help meet [suitable] for him." [23]*

2. Nothing had been created that was qualified to help the man. God brought him all the animals but did not find the right helper for the man. When God said he would make a suitable helpmate, He was saying straight up that He had to create someone who would make the man something he could never be if he were left to himself. It was as though man had to recognize and name someone at his level!

Nothing on earth matched Adam until Eve	*"And out of the ground the LORD God formed every beast of the field, and every fowl of the air; and brought them unto Adam to see what he would call them: and whatsoever Adam called every living creature, that was the name thereof. And Adam gave names to all cattle, and to the fowl of the air, and to every beast of the field, but for Adam there was not found an help meet [suitable] for him." [24]*

[23] Genesis 2:18-23 KJV.
[24] Genesis 2:19-20 KJV.

3. God formed and shaped her from the substance of the man.

*Woman was made **from** the man and **for** the man*	*"And the LORD God caused a deep sleep to fall upon Adam and he slept: and he took one of his ribs, and closed up the flesh instead thereof; And the rib, which the LORD God had taken from man, made he a woman."*[25]

4. God presented the woman to the man as a wonderful gift.

God brought the woman	*". . . and brought her unto the man."*[26]

5. Adam saw immediately that she was someone at his level at last.

Adam said that "she shall be called woman," or a man with a womb, because she was taken out of man. He accepted her at a place of equality. She was not beneath him to be walked on, or above him to lord it over him. She was someone to be at his side as they went through life, fulfilling the will of God as one.

Flesh and bone with the man	*"And Adam said, This is now bone of my bones, and flesh of my flesh: she shall be called Woman, because she was taken out of Man."*[27]

6. The man committed to give up everything for his woman.

Man leaves his parents for his wife	*"Therefore shall a man leave his father and his mother, and shall cleave unto his wife: and they shall be one flesh."*[28]

7. God created the woman from *the man* and for *the man, as his Kingmaker.* God made the woman from the man. She was literally

---

[25] Genesis 2:21-22 KJV.
[26] Genesis 2:22 KJV.
[27] Genesis 2:23 KJV.
[28] Genesis 2:24 KJV.

part of the man from the beginning of her creation. They were one in purpose and destiny. She was created to be his Kingmaker.

| **Woman was created for the man** | *"Neither was the man created for the woman; but the woman for the man."[29]* |

8. Their creation modeled the future unity of a husband and wife, and the union of Christ and His Bride, the Church.

| **Modeling Christ and the Church** | *"Husbands, love your wives, even as Christ also loved the church, and gave himself for it."[30]* |

9. The man immediately committed himself to this awesome woman from God. He spoke of the future sacrifice all husbands would make for their women with these words:

| **Man's commitment to his woman** | *"Therefore shall a man leave his father and his mother, and shall cleave unto his wife: and they shall be one flesh."[31]* |

The woman formed from the substance of Adam and shaped by the hand of God was so awesome that the man immediately committed himself to giving up everything for her. He saw her, received her as someone sent from God, and made a commitment to be faithful: "I will not use you. I will give myself to you. I will leave my father and mother and cleave to you." And to God, he said, "Thank you, God, for giving her to me. I will make her first, after You, in my life." Adam did not have a mother and father, but when he committed himself to the woman God had given him, he set a standard for every future husband, modeling the union of Christ and the Church.

10. In marriage, the two become one. A husband and wife are the same substance before God, just as Mrs. Adam was one with Adam

---

[29] 1 Corinthians 11:8-9 KJV.
[30] Ephesians 5:25 KJV.
[31] Genesis 2:24 KJV.

before God made her. They are in union. They are in one accord, going forward together for life.

THE CHURCH—ANOTHER OF GOD'S GREAT IDEAS

1. The Church, Christ's woman, is also God's great idea.
The Church is created as a helper suitable for Christ—a Bride adorned for her Husband.

The Church prepared as a bride for her husband	*"And I John saw the holy city, new Jerusalem, coming down from God out of heaven, prepared as a bride adorned for her husband."*[32]

2. The Church was birthed from Jesus' side by blood and water.
We are a blood-birthed Church who makes Jesus King.

Hymns of the Church **Jesus bought the Church with His blood**	*"The Church's one foundation Is Jesus Christ her Lord, She is His new creation By water and the Word. From heaven He came and sought her To be His holy bride; With His own blood He bought her And for her life He died."*[33]

The Church comes from Jesus' side, and the first woman came from Adam's side.

The Church comes from Jesus' side	*"But one of the soldiers with a spear pierced his side, and forthwith came there out blood and water."*[34]

---

[32] Revelation 21:2 KJV.
[33] Samuel J. Stone, "The Church's One Foundation" in *Lyra Fidelium; Twelve Hymns of the Twelve Articles of the Apostle's Creed* (London: Messrs. Parker and Co., 1866). Online at http://www.cyberhymnal.org/htm/c/h/chofound.htm.
[34] John 19:34 KJV.

| *The woman came from Adam's side* | *"And the Lord God caused a deep sleep to fall upon Adam and he slept: and he took one of his ribs [or his side], and closed up the flesh instead thereof; And the rib, which the Lord God had taken from man, made he a woman, and brought her unto the man. And Adam said, This is now bone of my bones, and flesh of my flesh: she shall be called Woman, because she was taken out of Man."[35]* |

3. The Church will be presented as a Bride to Jesus, just as Mrs. Adam was presented to Adam. In the same way that God presented a woman to Adam, He will also present the Church as a Bride to Christ. She will be glorious—without spot or wrinkle or any such thing, holy and without blemish[36]—and perfectly suitable for Him.

| *Bride without blemish, perfectly suited to Christ* | *"Husbands, love your wives, even as Christ also loved the church, and gave himself for it; That he might sanctify and cleanse it with the washing of water by the word, That he might present it to himself a glorious church, not having spot, or wrinkle, or any such thing; but that it should be holy and without blemish."[37]* |

4. The Church is not perfect yet, but is being perfected to marry the King.

| *Coming into perfection* | *"Till we all come in the unity of the faith, and of the knowledge of the Son of God, unto a perfect man, unto the measure of the stature of the fulness of Christ."[38]* |

---

[35] Genesis 2:21-23 KJV.
[36] Ephesians 5:27 KJV.
[37] Ephesians 5:25-27 KJV.
[38] Ephesians 4:13 KJV.

5. As Christ's woman, we are Kingmakers to Jesus, making Him known in the earth. Jesus is called "King of the saints." The saints make him King.

Singing His praises	*"And they sing the song of Moses the servant of God, and the song of the Lamb, saying, Great and marvellous are thy works, Lord God Almighty; just and true are thy ways, thou King of saints."[39]*

6. Jesus is your Husband. You voluntarily submit to Him as Lord. Jesus does not lord it over you as your Husband. You give him His place as Lord. He does not make you submit. You submit to your Lord voluntarily. Your Maker is your Husband.

The Lord is your Husband	*"For thy Maker is thine husband; the LORD of hosts is his name; and thy Redeemer the Holy One of Israel; The God of the whole earth shall he be called."[40]*

7. You love submitting to your King and His mission for your life. Submission means under the mission—"sub," meaning "under," and "mitting" meaning "mission." You are *under the mission of your King* when you submit to Jesus. You are fulfilling your assignment. You are obeying God voluntarily.

Submitting to His mission	*"Submit yourselves therefore to God. Resist the devil, and he will flee from you. Draw nigh to God, and he will draw nigh to you."[41]*

8. God has ordained that the relationship between a husband and wife would be an example of the relationship between Christ and the Church. Therefore, a woman submits to her husband as unto the Lord as a matter of principle, regardless of whether in her mind he

---

[39] Revelation 15:3 KJV.
[40] Isaiah 54:5 KJV.
[41] James 4:7-8 KJV.

deserves it or not, and regardless of what other women tell her. She listens to God.

Submitting to be an example of the Church	*"Wives, submit yourselves unto your own husbands, as unto the Lord. For the husband is the head of the wife, even as Christ is the head of the church: and he is the saviour of the body. Therefore as the church is subject unto Christ, so let the wives be to their own husbands in every thing."[42]*

9. Jesus died in the flesh *for all mankind*. Therefore, *voluntary submission to another person honors God*. *Godly submission is voluntarily dying* to your flesh *for the sake of others.* Jesus is our example. He died for us while we were yet sinners.

Voluntary submission makes us like Christ	*"For scarcely for a righteous man will one die; yet perhaps for a good man someone would even dare to die. But God demonstrates His own love toward us, in that while we were still sinners, Christ died for us."[43]*

10. Kingmakers humble themselves for the sake of lifting up others, just as Jesus humbled Himself all the way to the cross to lift us to the Father. Maybe your husband or your boss is not at the level where he should be, but if you are a Kingmaker, you die to yourself by an act of your will. You *volitionally* submit to him. You *intentionally* submit. You choose to submit as an act of your *will* for the sake of demonstrating the higher purposes of God. Instead of putting him down, you decide to lift him up. You are a Kingmaker. You can die to your pride to please God.

---

[42] Ephesians 5:22-24 KJV.
[43] Romans 5:7-9 NKJV.

Jesus was obedient all the way to death	*"And being found in fashion as a man, he humbled himself, and became obedient unto death, even the death of the cross."[44]*

11. Humbling yourself to serve others as Jesus did takes you to a new level of Christ-likeness. When you make a commitment to submit to others out of respect to God and you serve them, something inside of you rises to a new level of Christ-likeness. You are able to move into a higher spiritual plane, and you can take others beyond where they are in their spiritual development. That is because you are not exalting yourself but going down under them, as Jesus went down under you. You're dying to yourself and coming alive in Christ. You're a Kingmaker.

When you choose to submit to people who are not at the level where they should be or at the level where you are, that is *voluntary humiliation*—just like Jesus. You may have just as much education as they have. You know how to work a business better than they do. You are more dedicated to God, yet you submit to them by choice. That is being a Kingmaker. It brings out your greatness and it brings out the greatness in others. Jesus came to lift others! You're a lifter!

When you're up to date in your repentance to God and in a right relationship with the Lord, the blessings of God come upon you, and you see beyond yourself and your situation and see others.

Your husband may be filled with pride and refuses to be humble or to treat you right, and yet you have compassion for his weaknesses instead of pity for yourself. You maintain your Christ-like humility, because you're a Kingmaker.

KINGMAKER WIFE AND MOTHER: ABIGAIL ADAMS

John Adams was the second president of the United States, and his son John Quincy Adams was the sixth. Behind these great men was a great woman, Abigail Adams. Historians recognize that her role as Kingmaker to her husband John and son John Quincy had an impact on the history of America and the world.

---

[44] Philippians 2:8 KJV.

Abigail Adams had little formal education as a child, like most girls of her era, but her parents encouraged her intellectual development and she maintained her zeal for knowledge throughout her life. In her day, a woman's role was usually limited to the duties of the home, but Abigail's role as a New England wife and mother allowed her to wield tremendous influence over the political careers of her husband and son during a remarkable fifty-four years of marriage.

During her husband's travels, Abigail was careful not to restrain her husband from his public duty for the sake of her own personal needs, but instead educated herself in the skills she needed to be his Kingmaker at home. She maintained the family property and raised well-educated children during her husband's absences that were necessitated by his international role in our nation's founding.

When young John Quincy was only *13* (four days before his 14th birthday), he entered America's foreign service himself. He was chosen to be the secretary and interpreter for Francis Dana, who had been sent to the city of St. Petersburg in Russia to represent the colonies in their war against England. John Quincy could already speak French fluently, and had many other abilities as well. A remarkable accomplishment and a tribute to his parents. John Quincy would gain renown as the lawyer who obtained the freedom of the escaped slaves of the *Amistad*, a dramatic encounter recorded in the film by that name.

Here is an early observation of his mother on the absurdity of keeping slaves in a nation fighting for freedom. It was written in one of her many letters to her husband John (with original misspellings common to that era).

Mother's views that influenced end of slavery Abigail Adams (1832-1916) *Wife and Mother of* *U.S. Presidents*	*"It allways appeard a most iniquitious Scheme to me—fight ourselfs for what we are daily robbing and plundering from those who have as good a right to freedom as we have. You know my mind upon this Subject."*[45]

---

[45] Abigail Adams to John Adams, 22 September 1774. Massachusetts Historical Society. Online at http://www.masshist.org/digitaladams/aea/cfm/doc.cfm?id=L17740922aa. Accessed July 2012.

At the end of his mother's life, John Quincy wrote a tribute to her that speaks volumes of her role as Kingmaker to his father.

Kingmakers In History

Abigail Adams
(1832-1916)

Tribute to his mother from a former President of the United States

> *"There is not a virtue that can abide in the female heart but it was the ornament of hers. She had been fifty-four years the delight of my father's heart, the sweetener of all his toils, the comforter of all his sorrows, the sharer and heightener of all his joys. It was but the last time when I saw my father that he told me . . . [that] through all the good report and evil report of the world, in all his struggles and in all his sorrows, the affectionate participation and cheering encouragement of his wife had been his never-failing support, without which he was sure he should never have lived through them."*[46]

That is the mark of a Kingmaker. That is what your family will say about you.

FOCUSED ON OTHERS

When you're a kingmaker wife, mother, minister, manager, teacher, or whatever, you give others everything you have—your time, your resources, your money, the information you have gathered over your lifetime. You serve them. You meet their needs. You speak words of destiny into their lives. You bless them and release them to understand their significance in the heart of God. You confirm the seeds of faith that God has sown into their hearts. You give them vision for their bright future ahead, and when they succeed, your reward is their success.

---

[46] Mitchell, Stewart, ed., *New Letters of Abigail Adams, 1788-1801,* Boston: Houghton Mifflin Co., 1947, p. xxxiii, quoted online at http://www.galegroup.com/free_resources/whm/bio/adams_a.htm. Accessed July 2012.

*While others are focused on themselves and their
own advancement, Kingmakers are focused on
others. They are great in the kingdom of God
because they serve others and help meet others'
needs, just like Jesus.*

Kingmakers are friends for all seasons, not fair-
weather friends. When someone has an off-season, that's
when Kingmakers show their stuff. They stand in the
sidelines and cheer! They stay in faith and tell others, "You
can do it!" Success for themselves and others is part of their
spiritual DNA.

When you're a wife, God wants to give you so much faith for
your husband that you believe he can change history. Remember that
Sarah wasn't a perfect wife to Abraham. She had weaknesses and
made mistakes, but she understood God's destiny for her husband
even when his character didn't measure up. Despite her personal
weaknesses, she consistently submitted to her husband "as unto the
Lord," thousands of years before Paul would ever write, "Wives,
submit yourselves unto your own husbands, as unto the Lord."[47]

When you're a Kingmaker Wife, you look your husband dead
in the eyes and say, "I was made for you. You were not made for me.
Just as God made the woman for Adam, He made me for you. I will
not fail God in my assignment, nor will I fail you. I was born to
succeed in my role as helpmate to you. I love you but I do not
receive my value from you. My value and my call were determined
by the One who made me. The same God Who made you as my
husband is the God Who made me as your wife. We have the same
God, but we have different assignments. You will succeed in your
assignment. I was born to assure you of that. As Sarah called
Abraham 'Lord,' I call you 'Lord.' As the first woman created was
called Mrs. Adam (Genesis 2:5), I'm proud to be called Mrs. ____
(your husband's last name). Because Eve had only one husband, I'll

---

[47] Ephesians 5:22 KJV.

have only one husband. You won't have two wives, and I won't have two husbands. This union is forever."

When you're a Kingmaker Momma, you tell your children, "You have the God-given potential to become a person who can change the world. God gave you to me. I will love you and give you everything I can to make you more like Jesus. My life is committed to seeing you become great in the eyes of God and man. You will succeed. I am dedicated to your success."

When you're a Kingmaker in the Marketplace you're a wonder! You say to your co-workers, "We're a great team. I'm called to make you great. I haven't succeeded in my assignment until I've qualified you to become better than I am at this job." You say to your boss, "I'll do everything in my power to make you look good in the eyes of your superiors. I take personal responsibility for helping you to become the most recognized and successful leader in this company. I'll serve you so that you can become all that you are called to be."

KINGMAKER CONFESSIONS
Speaking Boldly About Yourself
"David encouraged himself in the LORD his God."[48]

One day my wife looked at me and said, "Honey, being with you is like breathing. I can't live without you." Can you imagine someone saying that to me? It took my breath to hear her say I had that kind of value to her. There's power in a wife's words to her husband. *Your words can make someone's day.*

My wife has real power and influence over me with her words. Her words of approval can make me feel on top of the world, and her words of disapproval can deflate me in an instant, even if she is saying something that I need to hear.

I carry two pictures of her with me wherever I go. One shows her beautiful smile that first melted my heart in high school in

---

[48] 1 Samuel 30:6 KJV.

Germany more than four decades ago, and the other shows her
serious side—a steady gaze that pierces my heart. At any given
moment, I can reach into my Bible and pull out either one of those
two pictures I carry of my wife. If I'm delayed in a meeting when
I've promised to get home to her, I remember those two pictures.
Which face do I want to see when I get home? I want to see the face
of pleasure, and I want to hear her words of affirmation.

You probably remember something positive you heard from
your husband, your momma or daddy, or a teacher or a boss or a
friend—something so encouraging that it made you believe you
could become what they said about you. You loved hearing those
words, just as I love hearing my wife's affirmations, but the truth is
that you don't have to wait for others to affirm you. *You can affirm
yourself when you see yourself as God sees you.* You can confess
your own greatness.

Sometimes people think that God likes nothing better than
dogging them out all the time, just like some critical person in their
lives, but that's not true. Judgment is God's *strange* work.[49]
Encouragement is His normal work. He's there cheering you on! He
wants you to be blessed! With God, you can always get an "A" for
effort. Even if you don't get all the results just right, God sees your
heart. From time to time, you need to encourage yourself in the
Lord, just as David did.

David encouraged himself in the Lord	*"And David was greatly distressed; for the people spake of stoning him, because the soul of all the people was grieved, every man for his sons and for his daughters: but David encouraged himself in the LORD his God."*[50]

At the end of each chapter, I'll ask you to encourage yourself
in the Lord and declare *Kingmaker Confessions* like these over your
life. I'll encourage you to speak well of yourself, to declare your
own greatness. You need to be encouraged. You need to *see* yourself

---

[49] "For the LORD shall rise up as in mount Perazim, he shall be wroth as in the valley of Gibeon, that he
may do his work, his strange work; and bring to pass his act, his strange act" (Isaiah 28:21 KJV).
[50] 1 Samuel 30:6 KJV.

more as a Kingmaker and *speak* to yourself as a Kingmaker. *You are a Kingmaker!*

Go ahead and say it one time: *"I'm a Kingmaker."* Say it again. *"I'm a Kingmaker. I make other people great. I'm going to be like Jesus in season and out of season, because it's always in season to be Christ-like. Greatness does what greatness is. Greatness is inside of me. Therefore, I do great things for God.*

KINGMAKER ACTIONS
Blessed By Doing His Will
"a doer of the work . . . will be blessed."[51]

You convince yourself that you're a great Kingmaker who is pleasing God by confessing greatness over yourself. You also convince yourself that you're a Kingmaker who's pleasing God if you *do* some things that Kingmakers do. At the end of each chapter, you'll find a list of *Kingmaker Actions*. After you *say* the *Kingmaker Confessions*, you'll *do* the *Kingmaker Actions*.

First, you *declare* that you're a Kingmaker. You say, *"Kingmaker is what I am,"* because *being* precedes *doing*. Then, you *do the work* of a Kingmaker, because what you do is a product of who you are.

> ***Greatness does what greatness is.***
> ***You say, "I'm a Kingmaker."***
> ***Then you say, "I will do the Kingmaker Actions."***

As you say the *Kingmaker Confessions* and do the *Kingmaker Actions*, you'll become as bold as a lion in every area of your life, and God will be able to say about you what He said about Job. "Have you considered My servant Job, that there is none like him on the earth, a blameless and upright man, one who fears God and shuns evil?"[52]

---

[51] James 1:25 NKJV.
[52] Job 1:8 NKJV.

Now put your name in the Scripture from Job. When God speaks to the witnesses in Heaven, He can say, *"Have you seen my servant _____ [insert your name]? There is no one like her in all the earth."*

- Read Genesis Chapters 1, 2, and 3. How did Adam start? What opportunities did God give him? Why didn't he finish well? What lessons can you draw for your own life?
- Make a list of the people in your life for whom you are called to be a Kingmaker. Pray for them.
- Visualize plans God has for them to prosper, and formulate actions you can take that will help bring those plans to pass.

KINGMAKER PRAYER
Submitting It All To God
". . . not my will, but thine, be done."[53]

Each chapter will close with a Kingmaker Prayer. As you pray, think of the rooms of your heart as being filled with heavenly qualities like lovingkindness, tender mercy, unconditional love, and humility. You are God's house, His woman, His bride. You please Him because you are mostly like Him. You have a mansion in Heaven because there is a mansion in your heart. Worship Him. Enter into His greatness.

Father, I pray in Jesus' name, help me to see that the Kingdom of God is beyond my own understanding. I break through in faith now beyond all of the limits I have placed on Your ability to change me or change my situation. I come against all fear. I walk in victory. I want You to be able to say to the Son, "Get ready for the Bride in this generation." When the trumpet sounds, let me be the one, let my heart be the ground, let now be the time. Even so, Lord Jesus, come quickly. In Jesus' name I pray. Amen.

---

[53] Luke 22:42 KJV.

Chapter 2
Thinking Outside the Box

"For as the heavens are higher than the earth,
so are my ways higher than your ways,
and my thoughts than your thoughts."[1]

In order to understand the concept of Kingmakers, you have to step into a level of thinking that transcends the realm of time and space. You have to think outside the box. You have to stretch your mind so that you can think like God in that eternal realm that in actuality dominates over this earthly, temporary realm. Just as Jesus was *in this world* but He was *not of this world*, that's also where you belong—beyond the thought limitations *of this world*.

Jesus said, "I am from above"	*"And he said unto them, Ye are from beneath; I am from above: ye are of this world; I am not of this world."[2]*

Mary was a Kingmaker for her Son Jesus, but first she had to move in her mind to another realm. When the words spoken by the angel Gabriel came to Mary from God, they startled her. *She had to choose to allow God's thoughts to enter the womb of her ears.* In God's sight, this woman was qualified to hear a "God said." The word or the sperm or the seed of Jesus was conceived in the spiritual womb of her ears before it was conceived in her natural womb. The words were beyond her comprehension. *No one had ever heard anything like that before.* She had to move her mind outside the box. She had to receive that seed without stumbling over her own inability to understand what God was saying.

The word that came to Mary from the angel was a Spirit word. It related to the destiny of God inside her natural physical body. The seed of a child was planted in Mary's natural womb, but

---

[1] Isaiah 55:9 KJV.
[2] John 8:23 KJV.

not by a man. Jesus' conception was an immaculate conception from God's Spirit. She was to carry Him physically so that he would be birthed forth naturally. From the time he was a baby until he was *bar mitzvah' d* at twelve years of age, Mary was to lay a spiritual foundation that would allow Him to fulfill the will of God. The Lord saw something in this woman out of all the women on the earth that allowed Him to send the angel to speak to her of this destiny.

> *Every woman has been called to bring into existence*
> *the purposes of God. You are a physical, visible*
> *manifestation of an invisible intent from another*
> *world—the realm of God's Spirit. Start to see*
> *yourself that way! Think outside the box!*

YOU'RE FROM ANOTHER WORLD

The angel Gabriel spoke to Mary concerning Jesus that He would rule over the house of Jacob ("the supplanter") forever.

Jesus came to reign!	*"He shall be great, and shall be called the Son of the Highest: and the Lord God shall give unto him the throne of his father David: And he shall reign over the house of Jacob for ever."[3]*

Jacob means supplanter. Jesus would reign over the house of the supplanter spirit of Jacob—his inappropriate lifestyle and inappropriate character. Jesus shall never yield to the flesh.

His Kingdom has no end	*"And of his Kingdom there shall be no end."[4]*

In receiving Jesus, you have joined yourself to a godly Kingdom that will never end. Kingmakers receive an eternal revelation of the purpose of their natural existence here on earth that

---

[3] Luke 1:32-33 KJV.
[4] Luke 1:33 KJV.

is beyond their earthly life. You learn to see your life in the light of eternity, because the only thing that you're going to take with you out of this world is that which came from the eternal world. That's what motivated the author of *Uncle Tom's Cabin.*

Kingmakers In History **Harriet Beecher Stowe** (1811-1896) *Author of* Uncle Tom's Cabin	*In 1850, when Harriet Beecher Stowe was 39 years old, the North entered into an agreement to capture slaves escaping from the South. Provoked to anguish by the cruel captures that resulted from this Fugitive Slave Law, this daughter of the famous preacher Lyman Beecher cried out, "I will write something! I will write if I live!" The resulting work of fiction,* Uncle Tom's Cabin, *became an instant best-seller, and even today is well-known as a powerful anti-slavery work.*

You were created for the purposes of God.
What God is making you into eternally is
what your life is all about.

You have a prophetic advantage in being a woman. Regardless of what society might say, you're not at a disadvantage at all, because God decided in His mind that you would be female. No human can define you. You have already been defined by creative order and the determination of God. He made you *what* you are, and *who* you are, and there is unlimited potential in you right now. Even if you think differently, you know that you're significant because God said so and because God made you. The Bible says in Isaiah 9 that his Kingdom shall never end. What things in your life are never ending? What part of your thinking can be transferred into the next world? What words are you speaking that are such eternal words that came from God so you know that you will always talk the same way, both in time and eternity?

YOU'RE A KING, NOT JUST A KINGMAKER

You are a Kingmaker whom God is training to be a King. When you think of a King, you usually focus on gender. If you're a woman you say, "I'm not a King. I'm a queen." That's not eternity talking. That's earthly talk. When the Lord thinks about a King He thinks about a position of responsibility. God is not limited by gender. If you are a Christian, you're in training to be a King.

Reigning	*"And hast made us unto our God kings and*
as kings	*priests: and we shall reign on the earth."[5]*

Covering the Back of the King

We have a saying in the inner city that when you really watch out for your brother, you cover his back. You say, "I've got your back." That means anything from protecting him from a knife or gunshot to covering up his mistakes. As a Kingmaker, you may be a King in training but you're not focused mindlessly on your own ascension to rulership. You're covering somebody's back. You're committed to others' increase, also. You're unselfishly building up others even to your own hurt, because you're following the pattern of Jesus.

Women in the marketplace. When you're a Kingmaker, your boss looks great, and nobody knows it was you. You work late and come in early to make the business run smoothly, but you don't brag, and everyone wonders how you do it so well.

Married women. When a husband abdicates spiritual leadership in the home, even though he is called to be head of the house or King of the house, if you will, if he is not man enough, that spiritual leadership passes down to the woman who has the maturity to be responsible over spiritual things. He may be ordained by God to be the leader in his house, but if his wife has more of the life of Jesus and the character of God, she may be the one in charge. She may not be ordained to be. She may not have the assignment, but she is the one responsible enough to handle the call of the revelation of God.

Sad to say, men are usually not the ones praying for the children. They are not the ones to whom God spoke the word to

---

[5] Revelation 5:10 KJV.

submit and do things responsibly, but who got the message? The wife got it. She was praying for his salvation. She was praying for his children to be protected. He was not praying. He was working in the marketplace. Then he was hanging out with the guys. He was in the gym. He was a man physically but you can be a male by gender and not be a man. Manhood relates to maturity. Maleness relates only to gender. Responsibility in God's eyes relates more to mature character than to gender. In some families, the man has been missing in spiritual and natural leadership, so one way that God can restore creative order in the home is for the woman to become a Kingmaker. She may have to function temporarily as a King, but all the time she's looking for ways to lift up her husband to be more kingly.

Single women in ministry. God is calling single women in the Church to come up another level. The Lord is looking to you. Others need your help now! The Church isn't just a physical building. The Church is people. Can you tell me where the Church begins and where it ends? Can you tell me what walls can keep you in? Is there a limitation on you? In reality, the Church is what you are. That's why you as a Kingmaker have to bring forth leaders in a generation still childish in its mentality.

LIKE JESUS BY CONVICTION AND FEAR OF GOD

Storms, earthquakes, and the tsunami cause people to become fearful, but the wind or quake that matters is not what occurs in the physical earth. *It is the fear of God* from the shaking that is now hitting the earth according to the signs in Mathew 24. God is bringing cataclysmic acts of nature to get us more serious about holiness than we have been with our little "christianette" mentality. It's time for us as a Church to grow up and become Christ's woman—people who understand creative order and are ruled by righteous convictions that are grounded in God's holiness.

Holiness is a *conviction* with Kingmakers, not just a preference. Holiness is living every day according to the convictions that come from God. It is the standard that God has set for the Church. We can talk about all our money that comes from God because of our faith. That's wonderful. We can be grateful for a large house or the fact that we own a company—that's all exciting. But hearing Jesus say these words to you, "Well done my good and faithful servant" after a life of living by your convictions, that affirmation has the greatest worth. That quality distinguishes a King in the Kingdom.

Becoming people of endurance through catastrophes	*"And you will hear of wars and threats of wars, but don't panic. Yes, these things must take place, but the end won't follow immediately. Nation will go to war against nation, and kingdom against kingdom. There will be famines and earthquakes in many parts of the world. But all this is only the first of the birth pains, with more to come. . . . But the one who endures to the end will be saved."[6]*

You are the King that God is making.
Say that, "I'm the King whom God is making!"
Maturity is coming to the body of Christ. Sobriety is coming. Holy standards are coming, and those standards are inside of you. You are not going to fall for counterfeit Christianity and false leadership. You are not going to resist God and set your own agenda. You're going to embrace God and all that He created you to be.

Submitting to God by Becoming Like Jesus

The only way that men and women can fulfill their God-created destiny is to become like Jesus. Jesus submitted to the Father all the way to the point of death. Can you do that? Can you die to the debates in your mind that go against God? Can you accept your role as a woman without trying to become a man?

When you read in 1 Peter 3 "Likewise, ye wives be in subjection," you can respond with resistance or you can respond with revelation. The Bible is a book of revelation. Expand your mind to embrace an understanding of subjection because it refers back to Jesus, Who subjected Himself to the will of God and bore our sins on the cross. *Being in subjection is being like Jesus.*

---

[6] Matthew 24:6-8, 13 NLT.

Subjected to righteousness	*"Who his own self bare our sins in his own body on the tree, that we, being dead to sins, should live unto righteousness: by whose stripes ye were healed."[7]*

Jesus voluntarily came down to earth, even though He had not sinned, and died for us, the Church. He carried us on His shoulders—meaning He carried us on His integrity, on His righteousness—*by lifting us*. He carried us on His resurrection to the Father. Jesus did not carry us to the Father from above us, but He carried us from up under us. He went down into hell and there defeated death, hell, and the grave. There a righteous man died unjustly, but He carried our sins on His shoulders. From up under us He lifted us up to the Father.

Kingmakers In History ***Catherine Booth*** (1832-1916) *Co-founder of the Salvation Army*	*"As I look back on life I do not remember the houses I have lived in, the people that I have known, the things of passing interest at the moment. They are all gone. There is nothing stands out before my mind as of any consequence, but the work I have done for God and Eternity."[8]*

A woman in ministry carries souls to Jesus. The lost can't save themselves, but God and His ministers bring them to the Lord. Catherine Booth and her husband William founded the Salvation Army in a time of great social upheaval when hardly anyone was meeting the spiritual or natural needs of the poor. At great personal cost, she labored her entire life on behalf of bringing others to the Savior. She never regretted it, but instead looked back with joy that she had chosen what was most important in life—serving others.

A wife carries her husband from up under him, like Jesus. In the same way that Jesus carries us, a wife goes down and carries her husband from up under him. She lifts him to a place of

---

[7] 1 Peter 2:24 KJV.
[8] Mildred Duff, *Catherine Booth: A Sketch*, with preface by General Bramwell Booth. Originally published by Salvation Army Book Department, circa 1907. Online at http://www.gutenberg.net/dirs/etext04/7cbth10h.htm. Accessed July 2012.

responsibility. A man is not a King until a wife voluntarily goes down and submits to him. He can't make her serve or submit.

> *She has to see by revelation the*
> *whole area of <u>sub-mission</u> as coming*
> *<u>under the mission</u> of God, just like Jesus.*

She goes to the place of submission not because her husband is great and he deserves it. She does it because God is great, and He deserves to be honored by her obedience to God's command that "Wives be in submission to your own husbands."

Submitted to husbands as the Church submits to Christ	*"Wives, submit yourselves unto your own husbands, as unto the Lord. For the husband is the head of the wife, even as Christ is the head of the church: and he is the saviour of the body."[9]*

A woman in the marketplace lifts others up. Good managers give others self-confidence by managing well without taking the credit, whether they are managing those below them or those above them in rank. When you see by revelation that "sub-mission" means "under the mission of God," you can understand that you become a Kingmaker when you come under the mission of God by submitting to those in authority. Your manager may have totally abdicated from her responsibilities, but when you become a Kingmaker, she becomes all that she can be in manifestation because of your commitment to serve her out of reverence for God.

WHY WOMEN ARE SO STRONG

This book will help you to understand the significance of your call as a woman from the perspective of Heaven in a way that you may not have seen from the perspective of earth. You're about to understand why you are disciplined. Why you have consistent

---

[9] Ephesians 5:22-23 KJV.

prayer times. Why you keep the character of Christ when others resist you. You'll see how you can make others great—in spite of themselves! Do you know why you're so strong? So consistent? Do you know why you're not thrown off by gender issues?

Because you're more than a woman by gender.
You're a holy woman of God.
Your femininity represents something
greater than most of the world can see.
You represent the Bride of Christ, the Church.

Maybe you've used your mouth the wrong way. Maybe you've said things that were not from God. Maybe you fussed at others too much to bring them into place. Where you need to repent, just repent and move on. Now you see your calling. *You're a Kingmaker.* Kingmaking is not for the wishy-washy or double-minded. It's not a one-time event, a once-a-week date night, or a monthly prayer time. *It's a day in, day out, consistent commitment to treat people the way you should treat Jesus, and the way Jesus treats you.* It doesn't matter whether you think they deserve it or not, because you're a Kingmaker.

Kingmaking is a commitment to give others honor,
respect, and encouragement.
It's doing something for even "the least of these" as
if you were doing it for Jesus.

Righteous toward the weak	*"Then the righteous will answer Him, saying, 'Lord, when did we see You hungry and feed You, or thirsty and give You drink? When did we see You a stranger and take You in, or naked and clothe You? Or when did we see You sick, or in prison, and come to You?' And the King will answer and say to them, 'Assuredly, I say to you, inasmuch as you did it to one of the least of these My brethren, you did it to Me.'"[10]*

---

[10] Matthew 25:37-40 NKJV.

IT'S THE SEASON OF YOUR SIGNIFICANCE

Kingmaking is a commitment to stay unselfish and connected to God in the midst of your relationship challenges because your unconditional love and fervent prayers will have a real impact on others' lives. Let the substance of God rise up inside of you. Give yourself to something larger than yourself. It's the season of your significance. Significance says, "I can be mistreated and still be Christ-like to my husband because my covenant was not a conditional covenant. It was for life. Even if he won't be like Christ, I will. Maybe he doesn't deserve sex, but I don't deserve salvation. I'm going to have sex with him instead of shutting the bedroom door on him because I made a covenant with God. I'm going to be like Jesus regardless of whether he is like Jesus or he isn't. *I'm going to be like Jesus in season and out of season, because it's always in season to be Christ-like.*

Feeling significant from valuing others	*"Don't be selfish; don't try to impress others. Be humble, thinking of others as better than yourselves. Don't look out only for your own interests, but take an interest in others, too."[11]*

Carrier of the Presence of Jesus
The driving motivation that sets a Kingmaker apart from the crowd is that she has made Jesus King in her life, and she does what *He* tells her to do—not her emotions or her critical friends. In Revelation, Jesus is called "King of saints." [12] A Kingmaker gives Jesus His rightful place as King in her life. She has met Him in a real way. She worships Him. She yields to His Lordship. She obeys Him. She tries to become more like Him. When a Kingmaker walks into a room, her presence speaks of Christ-likeness. You can tell she's been with Jesus. [13]

---

[11] Philippians 2:3-4 NLT.
[12] See Revelation 15:3.
[13] See Acts 4:13.

IT'S ALL ABOUT PLEASING GOD

In this book you will read many practical applications of the concept of Kingmakers, but I want to warn you—this is a spiritual book. You've heard the phrase "You're so heavenly minded that you're no earthly good." However, the opposite is true. If you're earthly minded, you don't look good in Heaven. When you understand the importance of spiritual principles that God has put in the earth since creation, you *are* earthly good. When you understand God's divine purpose for you as a woman in your marriage, parenthood, or career, you don't live for temporary, earthly rewards. You live for eternal rewards!

You must be motivated by the Spirit of God and His principles and truth to have real success in the home and everywhere else. It's not enough just to be driven by earthly success. Examine your heart motivations to see if they're in line with God, and if you're eligible for rewards in Heaven.

Why should you *want* to be a good wife?
Why should you *want* to be a good mother?
Why should you serve your family or your church?
Why should you be the top performer on your job?
Is it all about money? Position? Power? Sex?
No! It's all about God and life in His Kingdom.

Most women know on some level that God wants them to be good wives and mothers. Women in ministry want to reach and help people in obedience to their call. Marketplace women know that God wants them to excel in their position. When you try to do well but keep facing challenges head on, it can be tempting to get discouraged and give up—unless you're driven by a desire to please God. When you want to please Him, you press on because you understand that God has a purpose for your life and as you walk in that, His purpose will be fulfilled.

Fulfilled by God's Purpose in You

When you seek to please God, you're motivated by a supernatural sense of His purpose, which is even stronger than just "feeling His presence." God's divine purpose gives you a lot more staying power than goose bumps or a sense of obligation or a drive to be successful. When you reach the top, there's no empty feeling of "Is this all there is?" There's joy!

When you have a vision from God for your life and submit to it, His vision becomes a reality. God's vision for you relates to your creative purpose. God wants you to be like Christ in every area of your life. He is guiding you by the Holy Spirit into all truth about yourself. He shows you your weak areas, then gives you the strength to change. His encouragement gives you a sense of victory, because you know that He's pleased.

As a woman, it's naturally important to please your congregation, your staff, your husband, your parents and children and others in your life, but sometimes you can't satisfy any of them, no matter what you do. Pleasing people can never give you the consistent sense of acceptance that you get from pleasing God. Only God can give you fulfillment. When you are fulfilled, you can bless others and make *them* feel fulfilled.

KINGMAKER CONFESSIONS
Speaking Boldly About Yourself
"David encouraged himself in the LORD his God." [14]

Repeat these words until you believe them!

- The reality of God's Spirit and power have come to me today. I am good ground for what God is saying.
- I'm being transformed by God as Christ's woman, the Church. I'm dressed with His grace and favor. I'm awesome.
- I'm being brought to the place called glory.
- God's divine favor has been granted to me through Jesus Christ. I'll be fit to marry the Son.
- Because God's favor is on me, it will cause others around me to prosper.

---

[14] 1 Samuel 30:6 KJV.

- I have revelation for others. I am in agreement with God that the Word of God and the favor of God will be activated in others' lives.

God has good plans for you

" 'For I know the plans I have for you,' says the Lord. 'They are plans for good and not for disaster, to give you a future and a hope. In those days when you pray, I will listen. If you look for me in earnest, you will find me when you seek me.' "[15]

KINGMAKER ACTIONS
Blessed By Doing His Will
". . . a doer of the work will be blessed."[16]

I believe that as you read this book you'll begin to believe that you can become this Kingmaker. You can win this race that is set before you. You can see yourself as a genuine Kingmaker. Your words will be full of life. You'll have God-confidence. You'll make a genuine difference in people's lives. You'll have beauty so extravagant that people will notice you—not on the basis of your outward appearance, but from the beauty that shines from within.

- Read 1 Chronicles 16:29, a Scripture on the beauty of holiness.
- List ways that you can walk out the beauty of holiness in your daily life this week.
- What can you do that would make Jesus want to point to your life as an example for the Church to follow?
- Read 1 Peter 3:3-4. What do you look like in the hidden man of your heart?

---

[15] Jeremiah 29:11-13 NLT.
[16] See James 1:25.

KINGMAKER PRAYER
Submitting It All To God
" . . . not my will, but thine, be done."[17]

When God opens your eyes, you can break through the boundaries of your unbelief. You can press past your circumstances and your experience. You can move beyond the limitations of your own mind. Suddenly it seems possible that you can change and others can change, also. Instead of staying trapped inside the limits that you have placed on your life, pray. Submit it all to God. He will give you the keys to your future.

Father, in Jesus' name, help me to move outside the box in my thinking. Let me begin to live on the edge, to live in extreme faith. I rebuke mediocrity in the name of the Lord. I cancel every assignment of commonality where I would fall back and just be average. *There is something about me that relates to the greatness of God.* I call it forth now in the name of the Lord Jesus. I cancel every assignment of the devil against me. I am called to be in the Holy Spirit's presence and to do the will of God—in Earth, as it is in Heaven. I'm called to esteem others more highly than myself, following Your example. Help me to be more like You. In Jesus' name I pray. Amen.

---

[17] Luke 22:42 KJV.

Chapter 3
Loving Jesus First

*"And Jesus answered and said to her, 'Martha, Martha, you are
worried and troubled about many things. But one thing is
needed, and Mary has chosen that good part,
which will not be taken away from her.'"[1]*

I remember one day when I had to travel to another city
where I was speaking. My wife was not going with me that day. She
was going to meet me later. I kissed her in the bedroom before I
went downstairs to leave for the airport, but she followed me
downstairs for a few parting words. I got in the car and drove away.
A few minutes later my cell phone rang.

"You didn't kiss me goodbye!" she said.

"But Baby," I said, "I did kiss you!"

She said, "You didn't kiss me downstairs before you went
out the door. I want you to come home so I can kiss you goodbye!"

Now, understand, I was already miles down the road when
she called me. If you have ever been to Atlanta, you know that the
traffic into the city at rush hour can be a serious challenge, but I was
so convicted by her need for me to kiss her goodbye *again* that I
turned around and went back.

When I got in the door my oldest son Jason was there. He
burst out, "I can't believe you came back!" He was so shocked that I
decided it was worth the trip, not only to show my wife that I loved
her but also to show my son how a husband loves his wife beyond
reason!

Being with God to Become like Him
One of the goals of my life is to be so devoted to God that I can be
like God without trying. That was how He created us in the
beginning. Adam was like that before the Fall. So was Mrs. Adam.

---

[1] Luke 10:38-42 KJV.

They were like God. They did what pleased God *by nature* because they were made in the image of God.

Being like God by nature	*"So God created man in his own image, in the image of God created he him; male and female created he them."*[2]

A Kingmaker who pleases God by nature doesn't have to think about whether or not she'll submit to King Jesus. A wife doesn't go through a lot of challenges when her husband doesn't measure up and she has to lift him up, because she's acting the same way that Jesus acts toward us. A mother, manager, or friend can be disappointed, yet remain Christ-like.

A Kingmaker loves others and serves them and prays for them even when they're below the standard, or they don't treat her as they should. She's just like Jesus in this example from Ephesians in the *Message* Bible.

God didn't lose His temper with us	*"It's a wonder God didn't lose his temper and do away with the whole lot of us. Instead, immense in mercy and with an incredible love, he embraced us. He took our sin-dead lives and made us alive in Christ. He did all this on his own, with no help from us! Then he picked us up and set us down in highest Heaven in company with Jesus, our Messiah."*[3]

How do you become qualified to sit down in Heaven in company with Jesus? How do you learn to guard your heart with all diligence[4] so that you don't say or do something that hurts your credibility as a Kingmaker?

You submit and sit at Jesus' feet, just like Mary.

---

[2] Genesis 1:27 KJV.
[3] Ephesians 2, *The Message.*
[4] Proverbs 4:23.

Biblical Kingmakers

Mary of Bethany

Sister of Martha and Lazarus

"Now it happened as they went that He entered a certain village; and a certain woman named Martha welcomed Him into her house. And she had a sister called Mary, who also sat at Jesus' feet and heard His word. But Martha was distracted with much serving, and she approached Him and said, 'Lord, do You not care that my sister has left me to serve alone? Therefore tell her to help me.'

"And Jesus answered and said to her, 'Martha, Martha, you are worried and troubled about many things. But one thing is needed, and Mary has chosen that good part, which will not be taken away from her.'"[5]

Mary wanted to submit to Jesus and sit at His feet. Do you?

Naturally like God's daughter before the Fall

If you had been in the Garden before the Fall, you could have been naturally like God as His daughter, but because of the Fall you have to work out your salvation[6] by making a conscious decision to set aside your work and sit at Jesus' feet. As a Christian, you grow in Christ-likeness by spending time with Him. You will be like Him.

We shall be like Him

"Behold, what manner of love the Father hath bestowed upon us, that we should be called the sons of God: therefore the world knoweth us not, because it knew him not. Beloved, now are we the sons of God, and it doth not yet appear what we shall be: but we know that, when he shall appear, we shall be like him; for we shall see him as he is."[7]

---

[5] Luke 10:38-42 NKJV.
[6] See Philippians 2:12.
[7] 1 John 3:1-2 KJV.

Why do you have to do all this work to be like Jesus? God could drop on you in a burst of discontinuity and remove all the troublesome people in your life, solve all your problems, and zap you into Christ-likeness. However, even though He can intervene in miraculous ways, many times He comes through as you seek Him faithfully in the midst of your trials through the Word of God and prayer. Your heart commitment to seek and submit to your King—the love of your life—gives you the love you need toward everybody else.

HELPING OTHERS BECAUSE I'M LIKE GOD

The Bible says that when God created the woman she was to be a helper to the man. Does that offend you? It shouldn't. You should never be offended or feel inferior because the Bible calls the woman a helper, because being a helper is being like God.

The Bible says that God is our help and shield.

God, our help and shield	*"Our soul waiteth for the LORD: he is our help and our shield."[8]*

The Bible says that God is our help and deliverer.

God, our help and deliverer	*"But I am poor and needy: make haste unto me, O God: thou art my help and my deliverer."[9]*

Jesus said He would send us a Helper, Holy Spirit.

God, our Helper	*"And I will pray the Father, and He will give you another Helper, that He may abide with you forever."[10]*

---

[8] Psalm 33:20 KJV.
[9] Psalm 70:5 KJV.
[10] John 14:16 NKJV.

*Jesus, the firstborn, loved us first, and as we follow
after Him as His brethren, we can learn to love
others as He does. What is a great way to show love?
By helping!*

It is a great honor to be so helpful to others that you are a Kingmaker at the level of God! It says in Romans, "For whom he did foreknow, he also did predestinate to be conformed to the image of his Son, that he might be the firstborn among many brethren."[11] Notice this phrase, "that he might be the firstborn among many brethren." You have a high calling on your life. Someone else's destiny depends on your fulfillment of God's will.

PRESSING TOWARD GODLY CHARACTER

How large is your vision for your life? Can you see yourself prospering? Can you embrace the reality of the high calling of God that affects the lives of others through your dedication? Press!

Pressing toward perfection	*"I press toward the mark for the prize of the high calling of God in Christ Jesus. Let us therefore, as many as be perfect, be thus minded."[12]*

Can you see yourself becoming perfected in your calling as a Kingmaker? Remember what God said to Abraham. "All that your eyes can see I have given you."[13] Whom do you see yourself becoming in Christ? What do you see yourself doing?

Read the stories listed for the Kingmakers in Scripture on the following page, and be encouraged about what a great woman of God like you can do.

---

[11] Romans 8:29 KJV.
[12] Philippians 3:14-15 KJV.
[13] See Genesis 13:14-15.

KINGMAKERS IN SCRIPTURE

Kingmaker	Scripture	Kingmaker Action
Abigail	1 Samuel 25: 1-44	Saved David from killing her husband Nabal in a rage.
Deborah	Judges 4-5	Helped lead army of Israel into war when Barak would not go alone.
Esther	Book of Esther	Jewish queen of the Persian king Ahasuerus who saved the Jews from a plot to destroy them by submitting to her uncle Mordecai.
Joanna, wife of Herod's steward	Luke 8:1-3	Provided for Jesus from her personal wealth.
Jochebed, Mother of Moses	Exodus 2:1-10 Exodus 6:20 Hebrews 11:23	Hid her baby Moses, the future leader of Israel, to save his life.
Mary of Bethany, sister of Lazarus	Luke 10:38-42 John 12:1-3	Sat at Jesus' feet, honoring His teachings. Washed Jesus' feet with her hair, anointing Him for burial.
Mary, mother of Jesus	Gospels	Submitted to God and conceived spiritual seed of the Son of God. Raised her Son in the nurture and admonition of the Lord.
Priscilla, wife of Aquila	Romans 16:3-5 Acts 18:2-3	Worked as a tentmaker with her husband. They provided lodging for the apostle Paul and pastored one of the early churches.
Mother of Samson	Judges 13:1-24	Submitted to the angel who brought word she would have a son.
Rahab, the harlot	Joshua 2:1-21 Joshua 6:17-25 Matthew 1:5 Hebrews 11:31 James 2:24-25	Saved the lives of the Hebrew spies sent out by Joshua. Ancestor of Jesus. Acknowledged as a great woman of faith.
Ruth	Book of Ruth	Kingmaker to her mother-in-law, Naomi. Submitted to Boaz, her benefactor and future husband.
Sarah	Genesis	Submitted to her husband Abraham, even when he twice sent her into a king's harem.

You may think about your call in terms of specific actions or accomplishments, but God thinks about your call in terms of character. How much can you handle at your present level? How much could you handle if you increased in the substance of Christ? What great things could a holy woman do? What could a consecrated woman handle? What could somebody accomplish whose life is given over to God? How about you being that person?

Oral Roberts said he believes that the things that God allowed him to do were not because he was the first one called. He believes that someone else was called first to be the healing evangelist for his day, but that the Lord allowed him to take somebody else's place who was not faithful.

God will not have to say that you were unfaithful to your call and someone else had to take your place.

You're the one. Say, *"I'm the one!"*

When Jesus comes, you'll be excited about His coming because you have inside of you the grace of God. You can't wait for Him to come—not because you have escaped your desperate circumstances but because you've tasted of the world to come through your dedication.

You'll Love Heaven—It's just like you!

When you're caught up to be with Jesus in the air, absent from the body and present with the Lord,[14] you'll love Heaven, because everything on the inside of you perfectly matches it. If your time on earth comes to an end before Jesus comes, you'll still be carried up into Heaven rejoicing, because you have been brought into a reality of the Kingdom, and you know how to function in that realm.

In Heaven, there's humility. There's meekness. There's lovingkindness. There's patience, unconditional love, mercy, and longsuffering. All of that is furniture that's being made inside of you so that you'll be comfortable living there then.

When you get there and see how beautiful it is in Heaven, you'll see that it's not just a physical entity. It's a reality that relates to who you are. The reason you would not like hell is because you don't fit in there. There will be people who take revenge in hell.

---

[14] See 2 Corinthians 5:8.

There will be liars and adulterers and murderers and fornicators in hell, and that doesn't match your insides. You're full of light, so you don't go down into hell, which is full of darkness. You don't go there. You don't match. Hell wouldn't want you down there because your light would be a torment to the darkness of hell. You would be thrown out of hell because you don't belong there. It is nothing like you. You are full of truth and love and kindness. God is making you like Him, and you are yielding and submitting to what He tells you because "Thy people shall be willing in the day of thy power."[15]

SALVATION ARMY KINGMAKER: CATHERINE BOOTH

The Salvation Army was founded by William and Catherine Booth. They were such people of faith and so filled with the vision of God that they could see the potential in people whom others called the worst dregs of society. Their lives were dedicated to others' salvation. Catherine Booth was not only a Kingmaker to her husband, but also to the "least of these" whom Jesus calls us to serve. When she died at the age of sixty-one, after a life of dedication to others for the sake of Christ, she was without fear, ready for the next world, because she already knew it so well.

Kingmakers
In History

Catherine Booth
With her husband
William Co-Founders
of the Salvation Army

Words of faith as she
passed into Heaven

"My dear children and Friends, I have loved you so much, and in God's strength have helped you a little. Now, at His call, I am going away from you. The War must go on. Self-Denial will prove your love to Christ. All must do something. I send you my blessing. Fight on, and God be with you. Victory comes at last. I will meet you in Heaven."[16]

---

[15] Psalm 110:3 KJV.
[16] "Triumphant in Death," online at Salvation Army web site
http://www1.salvationarmy.org/heritage.nsf/0/4a30ecb11838235680256bbc0044636c?OpenDocument.
Accessed July 2012.

Her son Bramwell Booth wrote of his mother's passing:

> *"Soon after noon, I felt the deepening darkness of the long valley of the shadows was closing around my dear mother, and a little later I took my last farewell. Her lips moved, and she gave me one look of inexpressible tenderness and trust, which will live with me for ever. Again we sang:*
>
> *"My mistakes His free grace doth cover,*
> *My sins He doth wash away;*
> *These feet which shrink and falter*
> *Shall enter the Gates of Day."[17]*

Catherine Booth's son knew what it was to have a Kingmaker for a mother, and he saw her dedication to her family and her Lord continue to the end. That is what others will see in your life—to the end.

CREATING THE ENVIRONMENT OF HEAVEN IN YOUR HEART

How do you create the environment of Heaven like that in your heart? You hear God's voice every day in your times of fellowship with Him. You are submitted to a pastor. You are in fellowship with a local body. And you are reading God's Word for yourself every day.

When I travel from city to city, I sometimes ask members of churches where I visit to raise their hands if they read the Bible every day. In some of the most serious churches, not churches I would call religious or dead, the response is *less than ten percent.* That is not the way to become more like Christ. You may think you "know the Word," but if you aren't eating it daily, you'll be in trouble. The greatest chef who knows everything about food but doesn't eat any of it can still die of starvation!

---

[17] Ibid.

I challenge the members of the churches I oversee to go through seasons of saturating themselves with the Word of God by reading eight or more chapters a day. In my book *My Journey with God,* I challenge people to select at least one chapter a day from the Pentateuch, the historical books, wisdom books, prophets, poetry, Gospels, epistles and eschatological books, to build their understanding of broader Scriptural principles. Some Christians rely so heavily on Christian television that they are ignorant of the Bible for themselves. Now you must understand that I appear on Christian television, so I am by no means against it; and I thank God for the ministry that takes place through it. But many of the Christians who have been in the Lord for a while know good and well that TV can't feed them any better than eating fast food all the time would feed their body and help them grow!

I can just about guarantee that all of your faith declarations and spiritual visions will be robbed of much of their power if you aren't feeding your spirit the Word of God consistently. The life of a wife, mother, or full-time career woman can be very demanding, but that is all the more reason to take time for God. Many women burn out not because they "do too much" for other people, but because they don't stop long enough to take personal time with God. You can do it. You can make the sacrifice. It will be worth it.

COMMUNION, BAPTISM, AND THE SELF-LIFE

Two sacraments help explain the extreme Christ-like sacrifice of a Kingmaker on behalf of others. Those sacraments are communion and baptism. Both have elements of the death-life principle—they represent dying to self and living for Jesus.

It's amazing how much dying to self releases you to really live! After you die to self, you have no fear of death, but you also have no fear of what someone's words can do to hurt you. The Bible says of Jesus, "Death no longer has dominion over Him." Imagine how strong you would become if death had no power over you because you were walking in resurrection life. You could step outside a situation and look at it from Heaven's perspective, instead of getting caught up in the words and emotions of that moment. That is your reward. You are dead to sin and alive to God in Christ Jesus.

Alive to God in Christ Jesus

"Now if we died with Christ, we believe that we shall also live with Him, knowing that Christ, having been raised from the dead, dies no more. Death no longer has dominion over Him. For the death that He died, He died to sin once for all; but the life that He lives, He lives to God. Likewise you also, reckon yourselves to be dead indeed to sin, but alive to God in Christ Jesus our Lord."[18]

Communion and self-judgment

The Bible says to get all of your relationships right before you take communion. You die to the flesh so that you can be in communion with God as a wife, mother, manager, or minister on behalf of others. You could literally die if you ate the bread and drank the cup unworthily. How much better to die to your resentment than to be killed by God's wrath.

Taking time for self-examination

"Therefore whoever eats this bread or drinks this cup of the Lord in an unworthy manner will be guilty of the body and blood of the Lord. But let a man examine himself, and so let him eat of the bread and drink of the cup. For he who eats and drinks in an unworthy manner eats and drinks judgment to himself, not discerning the Lord's body. For this reason many are weak and sick among you, and many sleep."[19]

Jesus is perfect. He wants you perfect. If you can die to the flesh, He can commune with you at the level you need. Your husband or boss is not perfect, but when you die to the flesh you can relate to them at the level they need. Don't hold unforgiveness or resentment or any other sins against the people in your life. That disrupts your communion with God. The cost is too great. It's not worth the satisfaction you get from sulking. God makes it clear that

---

[18] Romans 6:8-11 NKJV.
[19] 1 Corinthians 11:27-31 NKJV.

you prove your love for Him by loving your neighbor, and who is your neighbor first if not your spouse or those in your close associations?

| *Taking time to love your neighbor* | *"Jesus said unto him, Thou shalt love the Lord thy God with all thy heart, and with all thy soul, and with all thy mind. This is the first and great commandment. And the second is like unto it, Thou shalt love thy neighbour as thyself. On these two commandments hang all the law and the prophets."*[20] |

When God's way prevails, the flesh-life suffers and dies. Good riddance! When you die to your flesh, you are on God's side and you can rejoice with Him.

Did you ever notice how much better you feel when you get over being hurt or angry? You can choose to get over it without anyone ever saying anything nice to you, just by an exercise of your will. That is how you make Jesus King—by laying yourself on the altar and embracing His will. Your relationships are the first place to demonstrate the power of that kind of obedience!

Communion creates a sense of intimacy with the Lord. I encourage you to take communion individually or, if you are married, as a couple or a family.

| *Taking time to take communion* | *"For as often as ye eat this bread, and drink this cup, ye do shew the Lord's death till he come."*[21] |

Of course, you understand that this means you remember Jesus' sacrifice for us on the Cross, but beyond that, it reminds you that you must partake of that death daily to be like Him. In taking communion, you are identifying with Christ's death and also with His resurrection. You are recalling your continual union with God

---

[20] Matthew 22:37-40 KJV.
[21] 1 Corinthians 11:26 KJV.

and your death to your own selfish desires, so that you can walk in
newness of life.

Walking in ***newness of life***	*"I am crucified with Christ: nevertheless I live; yet not I, but Christ liveth in me: and the life which I now live in the flesh I live by the faith of the Son of God, who loved me, and gave himself for me."*[22]

Jesus died for the sins of the world. Did you ever think about
the need for your own sacrifice and death to self on behalf of others?
You may never have to die *in the flesh* to be like Jesus, but you have
to die *to the flesh*. What attitudes would you have to change in order
to say that you had truly died to self? How willing are you to put up
with the punishment you get from other people in order to carry
them to God?

Baptism and identification with Jesus' death

Baptism gives public evidence of your initial commitment to Jesus
Christ, but the essence of baptism is your identification with Jesus'
death. That is bloodless martyrdom. Again, you don't die *in the flesh*
you die *to the flesh*. The Holy Spirit was sent down in Acts 1:8 to
give you the power to die *in the flesh* if you had to, but more
practically, to die *to the flesh*.

Receiving power ***to give up*** ***your rights***	*"But ye shall receive power, after that the Holy Ghost is come upon you: and ye shall be witnesses unto me both in Jerusalem, and in all Judaea, and in Samaria, and unto the uttermost part of the earth."*[23]

The word "witnesses" comes from a Greek word that means
"martyr." As we die to ourselves and obey the Lord's command to
go and make disciples of every nation, we literally bring the created
world into voluntarily loving and putting themselves in subjection to

---

[22] Galatians 2:20 KJV.
[23] Acts 1:8 KJV.

the Creator. As we teach them about baptism, we are also teaching
them about the blessings of dying to self and living for others.

**Empowered by
doing what
Jesus said**

*Jesus said, "All power is given unto me in
Heaven and in earth. Go ye therefore, and
teach all nations, baptizing them in the name of
the Father, and of the Son, and of the Holy
Ghost: Teaching them to observe all things
whatsoever I have commanded you: and, lo, I
am with you alway, even unto the end of the
world."[24]*

As a follower of Jesus, you express your love and subjection
to Christ in distinct ways. Submitting yourself to the Lord is
submitting yourself to His ways, His Word, and the husband or boss
He has given you. If you are a Mom, it is submitting your schedule
to your children's schedule in order to minister to their needs.

**Walking
in love**

*"Be . . . followers of God, as dear children; And
walk in love, as Christ also hath loved us, and
hath given himself for us an offering and a
sacrifice to God for a sweetsmelling savour."[25]*

Walking in love is a decision that takes God. You are
choosing a standard that in your natural mind you cannot possibly
keep. In your own ability, you can't love someone who is not always
loving toward you. With God's help, however, you can be quick to
forgive—not only as an act but also as an attitude of totally releasing
the other person who has wronged you. With God, you can keep
praying for someone in your life who has rejected God and your
godly counsel, as did one of the early church fathers, Augustine.
Because his mother Monica was a Kingmaker, he was saved, and
today we have the writings of this great man of God.

---

[24] Matthew 28:18-20 KJV.
[25] Ephesians 5:1-2 KJV.

MONICA: KINGMAKER MOTHER OF AUGUSTINE

Monica, the Kingmaker whose son Augustine would become one of the greatest leaders of the early Church, was born in the year 332 in North Africa, near Carthage, in what is now Tunisia. Her parents were devout Christians from noble families. However, Monica married a heathen, violent man who did not become born again until shortly before his death many years later. At the time of his death, their eldest son, Augustine, was seventeen. He was not following God, and soon went into total rebellion against the faith.

As he was to write later in his *Confessions*, his mother's faithfulness to pray for him and continue to share her faith with him, even when he moved in with a woman who bore him a child, were keys to his salvation. Monica was so persistent in asking the priests to pray for her son that they eventually began to avoid her. Before her death, she lived to see his conversion to the Savior she loved and served. Below are words of tribute that Augustine wrote of his mother after her death. He acknowledged that he never would have become a man of God without the prayers of his Kingmaker.

Kingmakers In History

Monica, Mother of Augustine
(332-387)

Augustine became one of the greatest theologians in the early history of the church, but not until his mother, Monica, had prayed for him for seventeen years to be saved. Here is what he said about his mother.

"For Thy hands, O my God, in the secret purpose of Thy providence, did not forsake my soul; and out of my mother's heart's blood, through her tears night and day poured out, was a sacrifice offered for me unto Thee; and Thou didst deal with me by wondrous ways. Thou didst it, O my God: for the steps of a man are ordered by the Lord, and He shall dispose his way. Or how shall we obtain salvation, but from Thy hand, re-making what it made?"

Augustine, *Confessions*[26]

---

[26] Augustine, *Confessions*, Book V. Online at http://www.classicallibrary.org/augustine/confessions/5.htm. Accessed July 2012.

Someday people will give praise to God for your dedication to pray and seek the Lord on their behalf. They will be so happy that you never gave up on them, regardless of how they treated you. As you are faithful to submit your life and your relationships to God, you build your ability and credibility to minister in your home and beyond your home. You receive power from being a martyr who has died to the flesh. God doesn't require you to put your ministry to your family first in your life as a limitation on you, but rather to empower you! Your faith in Jesus Christ is worked out in your relationships. It is a workout! It builds spiritual muscles just like running and lifting weights build natural muscles. You are being built up in God.

KINGMAKER CONFESSIONS
Speaking Boldly About Yourself
"David encouraged himself in the LORD his God."[27]

- I am becoming so devoted to God that I can be like God without trying.
- I am becoming like Jesus. I am a king in the making.
- I am a helper to _____ (make a list of names). I will not fail God in this assignment.
- I am a Kingmaker. I love others and serve them and pray for them even when they are below the standard, or they don't treat me as they should.

KINGMAKER ACTIONS
Blessed By Doing His Will
". . . a doer of the work will be blessed."[28]

- Redesign your prayer time to match the pattern in this chapter.
- Choose one of the examples of women in this chapter—from the Bible or from history—and apply her example to one of the relationships in your life.

---

[27] 1 Samuel 30:6 KJV.
[28] James 1:25 NKJV.

- Describe her obedience to His call on her life.
- List her godly character traits.
- Create a plan of action based on these traits.

KINGMAKER PRAYER
Submitting It All To God
" . . . not my will, but thine, be done."[29]

    The presence of God within you causes you to be changed into His image and likeness until you see only Jesus. You treat everyone the same. You love everybody the same. You value everybody the same. Jesus paid the same price for all of us. No one is worth more than anyone else. I believe that the Lord is raising up an authentic church that has been transformed into His image and likeness. Don't you yearn for full transformation? You can find that by loving Jesus first.

    When it comes to how much faith we have in prayer, we allow a lot of factors to control our minds. Don't let any outside influence control your thinking when it comes to believing God. When you practice knowing that Jesus loves you, you're in control. You can control everything else. Nothing can take you out of balance. Nothing can take you out of the nature of God and the character of Christ when you have faith.

Father, in Jesus' name, I bless You and thank You so much for Who You are. I thank You for this season of significance, for this time of looking at Your revelation of the total woman I am. I pray that You would open my eyes to see the revelation of who I am, both on a gender level and then at the level of that woman who excels them all—the Church. Father, help me to allow You to form me and to bring me into shape so that I might be the person You ordained me to be. Then help me to do what You ordained me to do. In the end, Lord, I want You to have the glory. Lord Jesus, I want You to say to me in that day, "Well done, my good and faithful servant."

---

[29] Luke 22:42 KJV.

Father, I want to be that Bride, that new Jerusalem who's made herself ready, who is clothed with white linen, who comes down from God out of Heaven, who will be perfectly suited for Your Son. I bless You and honor You now, in Jesus' name. Amen.

Chapter 4
The Scandal of Submission

"For they stumbled at that stumbling stone. As it is written: 'Behold, I lay in Zion a stumbling stone and rock of offense, and whoever believes on Him will not be put to shame.'"[1]

What the world is waiting to hear from Christians is not what you might think. It is not just a salvation message. It is not just miracles. The world is waiting for truth—a life-giving message that can be seen and read in your life. Christians have been afraid to give people the truth. We have thought that we had to become like them to win them, but we were wrong. It's time for the truth, even if it offends people, because that is what will set them free.

There are few areas that are as freeing and at the same time as scandalous in our day as the Bible's emphasis on submission to authority.

Wives don't want to submit to their husbands, and even go to the extent of keeping their daddy's name to show their independence.

Children don't want to submit to their parents, and they find willing partners in this rebellion in what they hear in school and watch on TV and the movies.

Church members disrespect their pastors.

Employees won't submit. Students won't submit. Terrorists won't submit. It is anarchy, because the Church is too ashamed to be the Church according to the Bible.

The world needs to see unashamed, genuine Christians walking out a lifestyle that is submitted to the Lordship of Jesus Christ and to all whom God has placed over them in lines of authority.

---

[1] Romans 9:32-33 NKJV.

SLAVE WOMAN'S SUBMISSION:
PHILLIS WHEATLEY

From what we know of slavery, it is amazing that anyone would submit to it and be able to express gratitude to God, but that was the testimony of Phillis Wheatley, who was stolen from Africa when she was a child of seven.

In 1761 Phillis *[that is the correct spelling of her name]* was purchased by a prominent tailor in Boston named John Wheatley as a servant for his wife. They taught her to read and write, and within sixteen months of her arrival in America she was reading passages from the Bible, Greek and Latin classics, astronomy, geography, history, and British literature. In 1767 she published her first poem in the Newport, Rhode Island, *Mercury,* but because of slavery in America the Wheatleys had to turn to London to find a publisher for her entire book of thirty-nine poems.

The title of the work was *Poems on Various Subjects, Religious and Moral.* It was the first volume of poetry to be published by a Black American.

Kingmakers In History **Phillis Wheatley** (1753-1784) *Poet, New England Slave*	*" 'TWAS mercy brought me from my Pagan land,* *Taught my benighted soul to understand* *That there's a God, that there's a Saviour too:* *Once I redemption neither sought nor knew,* *Some view our sable race with scornful eye,* *'Their colour is a diabolic die.'* *Remember, Christians, Negroes, black as Cain,* *May be refin'd, and join th' angelic train. "[2]*

---

[2] Phillis Wheatley, "On Being Brought from Africa to America," Online http://womenshistory.about.com/library/bio/blbio_phillis_wheatley_2.htm. Accessed July 2012.

In the Introduction is something unusual—the "attestation" that she had, indeed, written the poems herself:

"WE whose Names are underwritten, do assure the World, that the POEMS specified in the following Page, were (as we verily believe) written by Phillis, a young Negro Girl, who was but a few Years since, brought an uncultivated Barbarian from Africa, and has ever since been, and now is, under the Disadvantage of serving as a Slave in a Family in this Town. She has been examined by some of the best Judges, and is thought qualified to write them." [3]

WILLING TO BE MEEK FOR GOD

Phillis Wheatley's writings demonstrated that God is no respecter of persons.[4] He bestows His gifts on whom He will. He is not limited by our circumstances, and we should not be limited, either. Her poetry was a testimony to the truth of the call to meekness in the Scriptures, and so was her life.

Jesus said, "Blessed are the meek, for they shall inherit the earth." [5] The New Living Translation says it this way, "God blesses those who are gentle and lowly, for the whole earth will belong to them." [6] You're blessed when you allow God to give you a quiet spirit so that you never get out of control.

Many wives say to their husbands, "I'm not your slave." That puts you in opposition to the Bible. You'll be more fulfilled in your marriage if you decide to serve your husband and love doing it! When you serve for the sake of obedience to a principle of God, you're walking in real faith. You trust God to fulfill His Word as you serve. You don't worry about how this man will take advantage

---

[3] Seventeen prominent men gave their word that these poems were written by a slave. Online at http://womenshistory.about.com/library/bio/blbio_phillis_wheatley.htm. Accessed July 2012.
[4] See Acts 10:34.
[5] Matthew 5:5 KJV.
[6] Matthew 5:5 NLT.

of you if you serve him. You're demonstrating the meekness that shows up when someone is born of God. And then you get blessed!

Free to pursue what God wants for you

> *"Since Jesus went through everything you're going through and more, learn to think like him. Think of your sufferings as a weaning from that old sinful habit of always expecting to get your own way. Then you'll be able to live out your days free to pursue what God wants instead of being tyrannized by what you want."*[7]

When you live for others, the qualities of Christ-like meekness come alive inside of you. Then God can reach you, and He can teach you. He can give you His secrets. He can see that you have self-control so He can put you in control because He knows that you would never try to control others on the basis of your authority. You would never take advantage of anyone. You're a servant leader.

The way to become promotable is to take the low road. The fastest way for a wife to increase her influence in the home is by putting herself under her husband's authority. You will be promoted almost anywhere—ministry, marketplace, classroom—if you serve.

---

[7] 1 Peter 4:1-2, *The Message.*

You please God when you endure unfair treatment patiently, without retaliation, just as Jesus did

"You who are slaves must accept the authority of your masters. Do whatever they tell you—not only if they are kind and reasonable, but even if they are harsh. For God is pleased with you when, for the sake of your conscience, you patiently endure unfair treatment. Of course, you get no credit for being patient if you are beaten for doing wrong. But if you suffer for doing right and are patient beneath the blows, God is pleased with you.

"This suffering is all part of what God has called you to. Christ, who suffered for you, is your example. Follow in his steps. He never sinned, and he never deceived anyone. He did not retaliate when he was insulted. When he suffered, he did not threaten to get even. He left his case in the hands of God, who always judges fairly. He personally carried away our sins in his own body on the cross so we can be dead to sin and live for what is right."[8]

Remember that submission is an issue of God's sovereignty. It is something good! He established the picture of marriage according to His position as Creator. He declared that the wife would put herself under the mission of God. The Bible says, "Likewise ye wives be in submission to your husband"—under his mission or destiny. You are voluntarily coming under the destiny of God, because God decided the order of creation. He decided that a man would be created first and woman would follow as a helper suitable for him, and that is the model for Christ and the Church.

---

[8] 1 Peter 2:18-24 NLT.

You are called to cause a scandal by your obedience, just like Jesus

"This is the kind of life you've been invited into, the kind of life Christ lived. He suffered everything that came his way so you would know that it could be done, and also know how to do it, step-by-step.

"He never did one thing wrong, "Not once said anything amiss.

"They called him every name in the book and he said nothing back. He suffered in silence, content to let God set things right. He used his servant body to carry our sins to the Cross so we could be rid of sin, free to live the right way. His wounds became your healing. You were lost sheep with no idea who you were or where you were going. Now you're named and kept for good by the Shepherd of your souls." [9]

WILLING SUBMISSION—SHOCKING!

One of the most shocking experiences for an unbeliever is to see a woman willingly submit to her husband or someone in authority over her in the Church or the marketplace. *That is a scandal.* It's time for stirring people up with that kind of scandal! I believe that we will be on the verge of another great awakening when Christians are not afraid to look like Christ, act like Christ, and talk like Christ. His whole life was an example of voluntary humility and submission. You never once saw Him "fight the power." Even when He was arrested, mocked, and crucified, He embraced the calling on His life to accept what came.

In the coming awakening, I see the Church becoming so revived with the spirit of Christ-likeness—including the scandal of

---

[9] 1 Peter 2, *The Message.*

submission—that sinners will be converted in mass waves of repentance as they see our extreme faith.

One of the reasons that a sweeping worldwide revival has not happened for the past hundred years is that the world has not seen the manifestation of the life of Christ in most Christians.

God not only wants to reveal Himself *to you.* He also wants to reveal Himself *through you* for the sake of the world. That takes courage and a non-compromising spirit that unfortunately have been rare in the Church.

RADICAL CHRISTIAN LIVING

The apostle Paul said, "Ye are our epistle written in our hearts, known and read of all men."[10] What shows unbelievers that Jesus is real? They see in front of them an extraordinary group of people whose relationships with others exemplify the Spirit of Jesus—including submission.

The urgency of this message is increased by the reality that what we do in this world also has implications in the next. There is a future life for us, if we are born again. There is an eternal realm where we will rule and reign with Christ. God will determine your level then by what He observes now. Have you been faithful to follow His instructions? Then He can promote you. True promotion doesn't come from impressing people. That doesn't last. You want the favor enjoyed by Jesus—the favor that comes from God!

When you walk as Jesus walked, to some people, that is a scandal. It is unacceptable.
It doesn't fit the model of feminism that has become the standard for judging a woman's success. But it works!

---

[10] 2 Corinthians 3:2 KJV.

Jesus' Whole Life Was a Scandal

From the time that an unmarried woman conceived Jesus, His whole life was a scandal. He offended almost everyone. At the end of His earthly life, He was still offending people, and this time they were in a position to beat Him and crucify Him, yet He did not back down. He still chose to stay submitted, because that was the Father's way.

We have kept Christianity among Christians, but the Bible says that the Gentiles (the non-Jews, which relates to being among sinners) need to see shining examples of Christians. The Christian walk—the behavior of Christians—is something that shines among non-Christians, especially when it's something extreme, like unconditional love and the submission of God-fearing people to one another.

Seeing your good works, others glorify God	*". . . keep away from worldly desires that wage war against your very souls. Be careful to live properly among your unbelieving neighbors. Then even if they accuse you of doing wrong, they will see your honorable behavior, and they will give honor to God when he judges the world."[11]*

The challenges you face in your relationships with the people in your life are your proving ground where real Christianity can surface. It's actually your disagreements that demonstrate your Christ-like commitment, not your areas of agreement. Anybody can get along with someone who agrees with her all the time. God tests your Christian life by how you treat the person closest to you when that person provokes you and you don't raise up. That person is in the best position to see right through you, and so they are able to challenge the authenticity of your Christian life.

Whether you're talking to sinners about Christ or not, the Bible tells you to live His life before them. Others will see Christ in what you do even more than in what you say.

---

[11] 1 Peter 2:11-12 NLT.

If you are under God's authority, your love for others is not conditional based on how well they treat you or how many rights they give you. Christ-like love is sacrificial, not self-centered. It's an intensity of love, a lifestyle of love.

Everything you do in this life is on-the-job training for the next world. If your relationships are out of line, you prove that you would take advantage of God if He gave you authority in the eternal realm to rule over nations. The way that you dominate others reveals how you would dominate a nation. You prove your maturity first in your relationships. If a wife can't meet her husband's need for a loving, submitted wife, how can she meet the needs of God's Spirit?

Christians are called to astound the world with their Christ-like lives. Jesus was a Lamb slain. He had all power, but He used it only for others. He never used His power to prove His authority when someone challenged Him. He used His power to help others.

FROM CREATION TO CHRIST TO ETERNITY, IT'S RIGHT TO OBEY GOD

A godly woman is a woman who does things God's way. When God created man, He didn't create man as in gender. He created the whole human race. The woman was included in man. She was residing in Adam. God performed a divine operation on Adam to take something already in him to make a woman, but first He breathed into man the breath of life and he became a living soul.

The woman was made from the same substance. Adam was spirit. She was spirit. Adam was flesh. She was flesh. However, she was given a different responsibility. As a woman, you will not be judged *by the position* that God has given you; you'll be judged by *how responsible you are in that position.* In eternity, there will be no gender. If your husband is less faithful on earth than you are, he might be a shoe shine boy in your kingdom about a thousand miles over there in another world because he refuses to grow up and God can't trust him with great power.

God says if you'll be faithful with little, you'll be faithful with much. If you are faithful over the jurisdiction of the gender designation that God has given you, that makes you promotable. If you prove your qualities of Christ-likeness by submitting to your husband or those in authority or those who need you to help them, you qualify for authority in the next world.

Faithful over little, faithful over much	*"His lord said unto him, Well done, thou good and faithful servant: thou hast been faithful over a few things, I will make thee ruler over many things: enter thou into the joy of thy lord."*[12]

Does this offend you? That's because God is challenging you at your place of greatest resistance. He is a stumbling stone and a rock of offense. Just give in!

Jesus, a stumbling stone and rock of offense	*"For they stumbled at that stumbling stone. As it is written: 'Behold, I lay in Zion a stumbling stone and rock of offense, and whoever believes on Him will not be put to shame.'"*[13]

Your level of commitment becomes obvious by the degree to which you obey Him "outside the box" of your everyday thinking. Submission of wives to their husbands is one area where you have to get outside the box to understand it. Submission is a scandal and a stumbling block to those who don't comprehend its meaning in light of eternity.

Jesus, The *Skandalon*
Jesus is called a stumbling stone and a rock of offense. The English word "scandal" comes from the Greek word in that passage—*skandalon*. Jesus is the *Skandalon*. He asks us to do things like

---

[12] Matthew 25:21 KJV.
[13] Romans 9:32-33 NKJV.

wives submitting to their husbands that are outrageous, but are actually the key to life.

Many Christians will do anything to avoid scandals, even endorsing something that God calls an abomination just to keep peace. Jesus did not avoid scandals. *Jesus caused them.* Jesus did not come to submit to the world's ways but to break through to the people who were in the world and bring them into the reality of the Kingdom of Heaven in Earth. He challenged every other way of worldly thinking until people became broken and submitted to the Kingdom of God. Every kingdom submitted to the rock of offense became changed. Every kingdom that would not submit was crushed and broken in pieces.

Because God created man in His image and after His likeness, He has the absolute right to decide what is right for mankind. He can say what He wants, without explaining it to us. That's an area of sovereignty.

> *It doesn't matter to God if what He tells you to do causes a scandal. Just do it and be blessed.*

The issue of submission of a wife to her husband is a sovereignty issue. God is not apologizing for it. He is standing flat-footed. The submission scandal was already set in place when God created man first and then created woman second as a suitable helper. We don't have to understand why. He doesn't have to explain it to us. He declared it, and therefore it is so. Our responsibility is to accept it and walk in it, whether we understand it or not, because it's right, and it brings a blessing.

Mary Immediately Submitted

When God sent the angel Gabriel to tell Mary that she would give birth to His Son, Jesus, we know that she immediately submitted to the mission of God and received the seed of that word into her womb. She didn't laugh, as Sarah did.[14] She didn't debate. She just

---

[14] See Genesis 18:12.

yielded. She said, "Behold the handmaid of the Lord," [15] because she understood that God was the one speaking to her through the angel. When she said, "Be it unto me according to thy word"[16] she was saying, "I can and will do what you said. It shall come to pass as you said, because I'm going to obey You. I'm not going to refuse God." What if Mary had rebelled and rejected God's advances? He knew she wouldn't. That's why He chose her. He knew that she would yield to His mission.

I know a woman who served her husband faithfully and tirelessly, treating him like a king, even though he often over-indulged in alcohol. Eventually the pressure of his wife's submission was so great that he gave his life to the Lord and he hasn't looked back since! I remember how he would tell me that she actually called him "Lord" in the home. How do you think that made him feel? Puffed up? Larger than life? No, it humbled him tremendously. He even asked her to stop! Her genuine humility and willingness to subject herself to her husband broke him down! Not only do they enjoy a happy marriage, but also they and their children have been serving the Lord together for many years.

ABIGAIL: PREPARING DAVID TO BE KING

David had a wife named Abigail, whose name means "source of joy." Abigail was definitely a Kingmaker. Before Abigail was married to David, she was married to the ways of God. She had a Kingdom mentality. She stood for what was right because she saw what God was doing.

In 1 Samuel 25 is the story of how Abigail's husband Nabal refused to help David when he and his men, who were living in exile in the wilderness, came to him for food. Nabal's name means "fool." Why was he a fool? Because he didn't sow any of his resources into David—the new thing God was doing. Nabal had a wife who was a Kingmaker but he refused to be made into a king. He was the progeny of Caleb, who had said, "Give me my mountain"[17] in the

---

[15] Luke 1:38 KJV.
[16] Luke 1:38 KJV.
[17] See Joshua 14:12.

Promised Land when he was eighty years old, but Nabal didn't live off the substance of Caleb's legacy. He had a righteous wife, but he refused to receive the kingly substance of her life.

When David's men told him that Nabal had insulted them and refused to give them food, he was ready to go after Nabal and kill him and destroy his property. David was about to avenge himself, but then he met Abigail. She gave David and his men the food they needed, and also gave David some advice that saved him from doing something foolish that would have hurt his future kingship.

When David left and Abigail told Nabal what had happened, the Bible says Nabal became like a stone and in ten days he was dead. David said, "The Lord has revenged me." He called Abigail and said, "Come over here, girl. I want you to be my wife." Why? She was a Kingmaker.

Abigail warned David not to kill Nabal:

Abigail saved David from disqualifying himself as a king after God's heart

" 'When the Lord has done all he promised and has made you leader of Israel, don't let this be a blemish on your record. Then your conscience won't have to bear the staggering burden of needless bloodshed and vengeance. And when the Lord has done these great things for you, please remember me, your servant!'

"David replied to Abigail, 'Praise the Lord, the God of Israel, who has sent you to meet me today! Thank God for your good sense! Bless you for keeping me from murder and from carrying out vengeance with my own hands.' "[18]

---

[18] 1 Samuel 25:30-33 NLT.

When you read the very next chapter, 1 Samuel 26, you see that David discovered Saul asleep and could have killed him with his own spear and taken the kingdom from Saul by violence right then, but he said, "I refuse to touch God's anointed."[19]

Why? Abigail had already sown into him the kingly quality of not taking his own revenge. God, the One who had called him, was the One who was supposed to put him in the place where he should be. He said, "God will fight for me. Even though Saul is delivered into my hand, I can still go down even lower because a woman has shown me what I am supposed to be, and the level where I am supposed to walk, because she was a Kingmaker."

Are you a Kingmaker? What do you tell your husband that will help him to become a king? Do you urge him to be a rebel? "You're not going to let your boss treat you like that." "You can't give any more money to the pastor's vision." "You're always hanging around the church." Is what you are telling him making him more righteous? Is what you are telling him making him more of a man of God? Or is what you're telling him feeding his flesh because you are fleshly when you should be spiritual? Are you demanding a larger house? Are you pounding him about a new car? Are you insisting on more furniture? Even though your house is beautiful do you always want more?

You are not that kind of woman. You're a Kingmaker. Your focus is not on the natural realm. Your focus is on the spiritual realm. You're a Kingmaker. You're too awesome a woman of God to live for externals.

Maybe he doesn't make a lot of money, but he feels more like a man of God than someone who is a multi-billionaire. Why? You treat him like a multi-billionaire. You see him beyond where is and you treat him as what he will become.

HOW MICHAL MISSED IT

Marrying a king will not necessarily make you a Kingmaker. Michal, David's first wife, was married to the king of Israel, but

---

[19] See 1 Samuel 26:9.

because of her pride and her unwillingness to submit to the mission of God for her husband she missed partaking of the legacy that they should have built together.

When David brought the ark of God from the house of Obed-edom into the city of David, he was so excited that the Bible says, "David danced before the Lord with all his might; and David was girded with a linen ephod."[20] In effect, he took off all his clothes and barely had a covering around him. You cannot come before God with your clothes on. You have to come naked. That means you're transparent. You're vulnerable, with no hypocrisy.

Jesus Pictured Humiliation

Jesus was called David's greater son, and he was also a model of what it means to strip yourself. The last thing Jesus did was strip and put a towel around Himself and wash the disciples' feet.[21] He pictured humiliation. He humbled himself and washed the feet of someone He created. He was a picture of lowliness. The One who made you was coming down and eating a final supper with you and then washing your feet as the Creator and Sustainer of life, the Determiner of your future. Washing your feet! That is the model of humility that He gave the disciples.

David's worship was totally transparent. He was not trying to be kingly and maintain earthly regality. He was in the presence of God. In the presence of God I can get sloppy. In the presence of God I can break down. In the presence of God I'm not trying to speak proper English. In the presence of God I'm not trying to be something. I just realize that God is there and I'm going to strip myself of artificiality and give Him what's due to Him. That's what David did when He got back the Ark of the Covenant. It's too bad that David had a wife like Michal who could not appreciate his worship or his example of abandonment to God. She was far from a Kingmaker. She was more like a king-destroyer.

---

[20] 2 Samuel 6:14 KJV.
[21] See John 13:4.

Michal despised David's transparent worship

"So David and all the house of Israel brought up the ark of the LORD with shouting, and with the sound of the trumpet. And as the ark of the Lord came into the city of David, Michal Saul's daughter looked through a window, and saw king David leaping and dancing before the LORD; and she despised him in her heart." [22]

Saul's Daughter, not David's Wife

Notice not only that Michal despised her husband but also that she was called "Saul's daughter." Even though she was married to David, she was not called "David's wife." She still had her daddy's name. She preferred him over the new thing that God was doing in her life through her husband.

Today, Michal might have been a woman who had a hyphenated last name, or kept her own last name altogether. She wanted to bring her daddy's legacy into the new thing God was doing. She never in her heart became "David's wife." She stayed Saul's daughter. She was in rebellion against her true calling—to be submitted to God's mission for her husband as the king of Israel.

Saul was a symbol of the flesh. Saul was the people's choice. The whole time he was king he never sought after the Ark of God, the presence of God. He had no respect for spiritual things, and Michal was Saul's daughter, not David's wife.

Michal, Saul's daughter, was a symbol of someone who clung to her fleshly ways in the midst of an opportunity to become a part of something incredibly spiritual that God was doing in her husband. She was married to him physically, but she never put her agenda on the altar and submitted to her husband's destiny to be a man after God's own heart. [23] She was a consumer in her mentality, obsessed with the image and status that she expected her husband to provide for her. Her focus was completely on herself, and so she failed her man. That cost her dearly.

---

[22] 2 Samuel 6:15-16 KJV.
[23] See Acts 13:22.

David returned to bless his household	*"And as soon as David had made an end of offering burnt offerings and peace offerings, he blessed the people in the name of the Lord of hosts. . . . Then David returned to bless his household."[24]*

Now here we have a man of God coming from the presence of God to his wife and his household, to bless their socks off! What happened?

Michal disrespected and criticized her husband	*"Then David returned to bless his household. And Michal the daughter of Saul [notice that she was not called David's wife] came out to meet David, and said, 'How glorious was the king of Israel today, uncovering himself today in the eyes of the maids of his servants, as one of the base fellows shamelessly uncovers himself!'"[25]*

Did she say, "David, oh baby, you've been away to get the Ark of the Covenant. I saw you rejoicing and although I couldn't get with you to rejoice with you, I felt such love for you. You are such a good example"? No, that girl was not seeing that at all. She was married to him physically but she was not married into his destiny.

What are you doing, girl, talking to your husband like that? Now you call him "one of the vain fellows." You say there is no purpose in his worship of God. You say you see him as perverse because he worships God? You are more into the externals that come with the king's office than you are into what God is doing in the model of a man's heart.

Michal Cursed David When He Was Humble
She was talking about how he looked in the natural, but Jesus is dealing with the man as naked. David was to be a picture of vulnerability, not a man who would be perfect but a man who was

---

[24] 2 Samuel 6:18, 20 KJV.
[25] 2 Samuel 6:20 NKJV.

repentant; not a man who would do everything right but a man who would get it right once he found out he was wrong. She was more into correcting him than receiving his blessing and God's transformation.

David came to bless her, and Michal cursed her husband's worship! In her selfishness and self-consciousness, she was blind to his true intentions and his true heart. She couldn't receive what her husband wanted to give her because she was too carnal. She is like the wife who can quote Scripture and attend church, but at home everyone knows that you better watch out for her temper because she is still ruled by the flesh. Michal couldn't discern clearly what God was doing or saying to her, to her husband, or her household. She was not a Kingmaker.

God was shaping David into a picture of vulnerability. Dancing out of his clothes in worship symbolized shedding artificial covering and standing naked and vulnerable in the presence of God. Revolutionary!

Instead of being sensitive and loving in the face of his vulnerability, and welcoming him, she took advantage of his lowering his guard to stab him with her words. She was more into criticizing David than receiving the blessing and the transformation that God had in store for her.

The Bible says that a wife by her chaste manner of living may win her husband without a word.[26] God puts a supernatural way on a woman that she doesn't have to use her mouth at all to change people.

Some wives cut short their husband's message by not listening and running their mouths before the blessing can be spoken over them. Women can cause the same damage in ministry or marketplace, or they can be insensitive to their children's gentle attempts to express themselves and impatiently brush them away.

---

[26] See 1 Peter 3:1.

When you don't have a God said but you talk on and on anyway about what is happening in the natural, you speak not out of the supernatural but out of the flesh. You speak with the same authority as if you had been praying and fasting, but you are speaking not to make a king but to bring a king down.

David had just come from the worship of God, from His presence and the Ark of the Covenant to bless her and his house. Michal had the seed of her father, and she completely missed God in this. Here she had a husband who knew there was more to serving God than getting a big palace and lots of money, and she just didn't get it. She needed to get her daddy's seed off of her, but she refused to yield to her husband, who represented a different seed.

Michal paid a tremendous price for her fleshly insensitivity and refusal to submit to her husband as God had ordained. It should be a warning to every wife and an opportunity to see the way that wives should go to please God. Michal's spirit could not be reproduced, so her dynasty ended with her.

Barrenness of Michal, a rebellious woman

"Therefore Michal the daughter of Saul had no child unto the day of her death." [27]

---

[27] 2 Samuel 6:23 KJV.

How Michal Failed God As A Wife
". . . and she despised him in her heart."[28]

- She was married to a king, but she was not a Kingmaker.
- She carried her daddy's legacy into her marriage, and never submitted herself to the mission of God for her family under David.
- She despised her husband's vulnerability.
- She was ruled by the flesh.
- She was prideful.
- She could not discern her husband's heart.
- Her bad attitude kept her husband from blessing their house

---

The Bible repeats three times that Michal had no child until the day of her death. Why? She never came into the spiritual legacy of David. While David maintained the right attitude toward God, Michal did not. She refused to become David's wife in the truest sense, so God said, "I am not going to let the daughter of Saul, a picture of the flesh, bear children with somebody like David, who represents the new thing I am doing in the Spirit. I am not going to let Michal have children because they will have no regard for spiritual things. I am not going to bring back Saul's legacy. I am going to let David maintain his position of worship."

VOLUNTARY SUBMISSION PLEASES GOD

Nowhere is the husband permitted to force his wife to submit. His ability to function in headship in the home is completely dependent on her *decision* to submit.

The Bible's commandment to submit to your husband or those in authority hinges on the concept of <u>voluntary</u> submission. That is what makes it so powerful.

---

[28] 2 Samuel 6:16 KJV.

God Honored Sarah's Submission

Sarah was the total opposite of Michal. Sarah was a Kingmaker because she received the revelation of a divine mission given to her husband as her own. As a result, she was in a position to add to him the substance necessary for Abraham to be what God had called him to be. She went along with that as unto the Lord.

When she did it unto the Lord and not as unto Abraham the Lord heard it and God came to Egypt and visited him with the miracles of judgment from the Throne Room. God got a new dedication out of Pharaoh when the plague came on him, because he was messing with a woman who was staying in the position of reverence to her husband. She was a bridge to carry him somewhere in his off season, because she was a Kingmaker.

When You Marry Jesus, You Submit to Him

Michal was not submitted to David in any area that we know of. She was "Saul's daughter" when she should have been "David's wife." She had a hyphenated name. She respected her daddy more than she respected her husband. Many women today keep their daddy's names and their "professional names," but when the church of Jesus Christ gets born again, and you are espoused to Jesus, you change your name. You submit and carry His name.

You can't bring your daddy's name over into the Kingdom of God. You have to totally separate yourself from your old life. When you marry Jesus, you marry Him fully. You take His name. That means being in union with everything He is about.

Help Your Husband Out and Submit

Some wives today are out of position—not natural position, but spiritual position—because even though a man of God is a king to his people and a king to his leaders, where he is first called to be a king is to his own house. If you as his wife don't give him his rightful place, he is not half the man he could be, because he is authenticated first in his own house. If you don't do it willingly, then God has to come against you. He won't make you submit, but

He will come against you. I don't know about you, but I don't ever want to do anything that causes God to oppose me. So help a brother out and help yourself as well.

Even though God has given the man authority over the woman, everything in the Kingdom of God works voluntarily. Even if your husband had muscles as big as Hercules, even though he could make enough money to buy the Empire State Building, he could not make you submit. The only way your husband is the man in that house is that you voluntarily go up under him and let him do his thing because you're a Kingmaker.

The poor brother has been working all day long outside the home on the job. People have been banging on him. The workers are not working for him as they should. People are criticizing him. He is getting false accusations. He is not being treated as he should be treated. Want to do something great? Here's a picture of how you can make home like Heaven for that man:

He comes home and says, "Baby, I'm home."

You come up to the brother, and you say, "Baby, I'm so glad to see you!"

He says, "Honey, it was a rough day."

You grab the brother and you say, "Oh, baby, I'm so glad to see you." And you say, "Sit down here. Take your shoes off." And you start rubbing the brother's feet. Then you say, "Get ready now, Baby . I am going to fix you some tea. I'm getting dinner ready."

What is happening with that? Even though he is looked at as somebody underneath the standard outside, when he comes in the house he is now lifted up to another position—not because he makes himself a king, but because you make him a king. You go down under him.

He can't make you go low. You have just as much education as he has. You know how to work a business. If you're working out in the marketplace, you may be making more money than he makes. You're thinking while he's sleeping. He knows you're really greater than he is because there is something inside of you that is repentant toward God and right before the Lord, and so the blessings of God are all over you. And yet he still has that manly pride and ego. He refuses to be humble. He can't believe that as his wife, as his woman, you are going down under him just as Jesus went down and carried our sins on the cross.

Something supernatural is working in you and you are able to go down under him, under his walk. He's not at the level yet, but because you voluntarily go under him, he is moved to a position above you. Just as Jesus carried us on the cross and lifted us up to the Father, you go down under him and lift the brother up to be somebody when he feels like nobody. When outside they are treating him like a tramp, you're making him a king. He knows you're greater than he is. He knows you're smarter than he is. He knows you're reading the Word when he's giving excuses about being tired. He doesn't deserve to be treated like that. That's what messes him up and gets him changed!

Your meek and quiet spirit messes him up

"While they behold your chaste conversation coupled with fear. Whose adorning let it not be that outward adorning of plaiting the hair, and of wearing of gold, or of putting on of apparel; But let it be the hidden man of the heart, in that which is not corruptible, even the ornament of a meek and quiet spirit, which is in the sight of God of great price."[29]

He beholds your "chaste conversation coupled with fear." "Fear" in this context means you have the utmost respect for God's order. You are clothed with humility. You carry yourself with dignity as an honored wife. You respect him even though you can name ten times he didn't keep his word, and you know he is not praying as he should. You respect him even though you know he should be making more money in the house. You respect him even though your daddy took care of you better than he is taking care of you. Your respect isn't based on his performance. It's based on doing what God says. You're clothed in a gorgeous spirit that's worth more than gold, because it comes from God. "Don't be concerned about the outward beauty that depends on fancy hairstyles, expensive jewelry, or beautiful clothes. You should be known for the beauty that comes from within, the unfading beauty of a gentle and quiet spirit, which is so precious to God."

---

[29] 1 Peter 3:3-4 NLT.

Seeing Weaknesses Yet Submitting Takes Character
You know how to shut him down with a word because you're out-thinking him. You know he has not laid down a five-year plan. You know he hasn't planned out the vacation. You know he doesn't know how to manage money as he ought to manage money in the house. You know he handles himself better on the outside than he handles himself on the inside. Yet in view of all of that, you have a meek and a quiet spirit. You have subjected yourself. You are a Kingmaker! Just as Jesus carried the whole world on His shoulders, there is a strength inside of you to carry a man on your shoulders until he comes up to the level where he should be. The only place he can get respect is in his house.

DO YOU LOVE SUBMISSION?

I love the word subjection, because it is a strong word for building strong Christians. We love to hear about how "God *loves* you," but we also need to hear about how we ought to obey God, especially if it interferes with our own personal agenda. Subjection of wives to their husbands in 1 Peter 3:1 is the same word used in 1 Peter 2:18 where it says, "Servants, be subject to your masters with all fear." [30] That word "servants" also means "slaves." Wives be subject to your husbands as slaves are subject to their masters. Isn't that a scandal! We'd better not let that get out, or we will be attacked by every feminist! Actually, this word from the Bible is something that every feminist needs, because it's a liberating word. Every word of God is true. Jesus said that the truth sets us free. [31]

> *Women are subject to their husbands and slaves are subject to their masters in the same way that Christ was subject to the will of His Father. Subjection is a natural example of a spiritual attitude that comes from Christ.*

---

[30] 1 Peter 2:18 KJV.
[31] See John 8:32.

When we voluntarily go under someone, we are becoming Christ-like. *It doesn't get any better than that.* The New Living Translation uses the strong language of slavery that we need to hear to understand what Christ did for us, and what He is calling us to do for one another:

*We are
slaves of God,
like Christ*

> *"You who are slaves must accept the authority of your masters. . . . In the same way, you wives must accept the authority of your husbands, even those who refuse to accept the Good News. Your godly lives will speak to them better than any words. They will be won over by watching your pure, godly behavior."[32]*

With the influence of feminism on recent generations, I must clarify a few things that seem pretty obvious to me. Just as too many men today despise the biblical responsibility that comes with being a husband and father, many women despise the biblical charge to voluntarily submit to their husband's leadership. Their rationale is that this submission is opposed to gender equality, and reduces their value in comparison to their husbands. This has been one of the most successful deceptions of the devil to make marriages miserable and often destroy them altogether.

In the same way, women in the corporate world have allowed legitimate complaints about a glass ceiling that keeps them from advancing because of their gender to cause them to become aggressive against submitting to anyone—sometimes even God.

Submission is one scandal that has feminists angry at the Church, and it is not going away. You might as well face it head on: When you commit your life to the Lord Jesus Christ, you submit to his Lordship. When you commit to Jesus and do not submit to His Lordship, you are outside the domain of the Kingdom of Heaven.

When you commit to marrying your husband, you submit to him as head of the household, just as Christ is head of the Church. That's why you take his name. It's not O.K. to keep your daddy's name when you marry. It's not O.K. to maintain separate lives. You

---

[32] 1 Peter 2:18; 3:1-2 NLT.

are now one. You take your husband's name and submit to him. It's a scandal. It's the talk of the town. It's a model of Christ and the Church.

> *If submission were easy, every woman would embrace it, but it's not, and they don't. Submission is not for the faint-hearted, weak, or immature. Like all matters of faith, it separates the women from the girls. It's tested in conflict and disagreement.*

It's easier to submit to your husband when you agree with what he says. However, the depth of your submission to God is proven out when you disagree with your husband, but submit to him anyway out of reverence and respect for God.

> *A wife who understands submission does not submit because her husband is great; she submits because God is great.*

Women who submit willingly to their husbands will find their other efforts flowing in God's amazing grace. When they refuse to submit, their other efforts will be frustrated, and they may even find themselves cut off by God altogether. They may be trying, in some sense, to do God's *will*, but they forsake His *ways*.

Just as God wouldn't want to make you rich by enabling you to rob a bank, He is not trying to get you where He wants you by allowing you to usurp your husband's authority or rebel against someone's leadership. Women who do this ultimately miss their calling and their God-ordained road to greatness.

The marketplace is often the same: too many men and women claw, cheat and deceive their way to the top, and often find it empty when they get there. Too often, these women then act confused when greatness seems to pass them by!

ANN JUDSON—MISSIONARY KINGMAKER

On February 19, 1812, seven days after her marriage to Adoniram Judson, Ann Hasseltine Judson set sail for India. She was 23 years old. Once in India, because of persecution by the British occupation forces they left for Rangoon, Burma, the following year. Because of continuing oppression in Burma and the severity of the climate, they experienced severe trials and even after many years in their Baptist missionary work few native converts had been saved.

Kingmakers In History

Ann Hasseltine Judson
(1789-1826)

Prayer of a missionary to Burma

"I feel willing and expect, if nothing in providence prevents, to spend my days in this world in heathen lands. Yes, Lydia, I have about come to the determination to give up all my comforts and enjoyments here, sacrifice my affection to relatives and friends, and go where God, in his providence, shall see fit to place me. My determinations are not hasty, or formed without viewing the dangers, trials, and hardships attendant on a missionary life. Nor were my determinations formed in consequence of an attachment to an earthly object; but with a sense of my obligation to God, and a full conviction of its being a call in providence, and consequently my duty. . . . How short is time, how boundless is eternity! If we may be considered worthy to suffer for Jesus here, will it not enhance our happiness hereafter?"[33]

When Ann's husband was jailed under terrible conditions and nearly died, she relentlessly pursued the Burmese officials even though her own health was suffering. Finally, because of her efforts, he was released to preach the Gospel after nearly two years. Two months after his release she died and their only child died soon after.

However, her husband lived to see the fruit of the sacrifice of his Kingmaker wife. By the time of his death in 1850, he had

---

[33]Belle Marvel Brain (1859-1933), *Love Stories of Great Missionaries* (New York: Fleming H. Revel Company, 1913). "Winning a Wife in the Homeland," Pages 15-16.

translated the entire Bible into Burmese, and the pagan land of
Burma had sixty-three churches with 163 missionaries and native
church leaders. The Burmese church has survived the centuries in
spite of its predominantly Buddhist culture.

INCREASING INFLUENCE BY SUBMITTING

The reward of submission is influence over those to whom
you willingly submit and even more important—favor with God.
What you could never have gained by being a rebel intent on getting
your own way you will gain by obeying God and staying in the right
posture toward the person God has placed over you. You are no
longer relying on your own powers of seduction or rebellion to get
your own way. You are right in the center of the favor granted by
God to those who follow His ways. It might take longer to manifest
than a good pout or a screaming fit, but you will get your way, and
you will have the satisfaction of doing it right.

Finding favor through being righteous	*"For you bless the godly, O LORD; you surround them with your shield of love."[34]*

In the earth right now Jesus is only King of His Church in
manifestation to the degree that the Church submits to Him. It takes
voluntary submission by the Church to make Jesus King over His
Bride. Jesus does not force the Church to submit. Jesus is a King in
His character and power and position, but the Church makes Him
King in manifestation by submitting to His will voluntarily. That is
how the glory of God is ordained to cover the earth—through the
voluntary submission of the Church to Jesus.

Every Christian home is supposed to be a miniature version
of this, with the husband modeling Jesus, and the wife modeling the
Church. Every workplace should be a model of people submitting to
one another. Christians should shine like lamps on lamp stands in the
marketplace, filling their offices with peace and compassion.

---

[34] Psalm 5:12 NLT.

Just as an unsubmitted Church dishonors Christ, unsubmitted wives dishonor their husbands, and unsubmitted workers dishonor their managers. When you are out of your God-ordained position of humility in earthly relationships, you are out of your spiritual position with God, and everything suffers.

Embracing Christ-like Humility

Jesus is not only the King crowned by the Church. He also makes us kings with Him in the earth, and He does this from a position of subjection. Jesus voluntarily came down from Heaven and made Himself subject to the trials and experiences of being a human being. Jesus carried us from underneath. He went to hell and there defeated death, hell, and the grave. What happened to Him was "unfair," but it bought our salvation. As a result, God said that every knee must bow to Him.[35]

All Christians, male and female, single and married, need to embrace this aspect of Christ-likeness to increase their influence. Christian wives who are married to unsaved or carnal husbands become Kingmakers by becoming Christ-like. Gifted people model Christ by submitting their talents and gifts to Him. This is beyond gender, and beyond your position or role in your home or the marketplace. This is a spiritual reality.

The spiritual reality is that, as a Christian, you are modeling Jesus to everyone, including your employees, your boss, your co-workers and your family and pastor. Your voluntary submission and subjection to authority shows the power and reality of Jesus in you. It may be an unjust situation, just as it was unfair for Jesus, but just as for Jesus the result of temporary subjection will be eternal rewards.[36]

Christian women must never forget that their call to be like Jesus is equal to that of Christian men. Women have the same ability as men to please God, become like Him, and gain rewards in Heaven. It is an honor for us as believers to be able to show forth Christ-likeness in the earth.

---

[35] See Philippians 2:10.
[36] See Luke 6:23.

Ultimately, you are called to make your husband or boss something he could never be on his own. It isn't that it's all "about him." It's that you're like Jesus, and Jesus makes you into something that you could never be on your own.

ANNA THE PROPHETESS: SUBMITTED SINGLE

All of the principles of submission are applicable to the Christian life in general, not just married life. Single Christian women are already married to Jesus, and should carry themselves that way.

As you are reading this book, I hope you will walk away with real revelation that will be useful to you now and in the future. You will find a lot of applications to Kingmakers who are married because I want you to get a picture of how spiritually significant marriage is.

If you are single, you need to understand submission in the context of marriage even if you don't plan to be married someday. Every Christian must understand the biblical model of marriage because of God's creative order that began in Genesis, and the relationship of Christ and the Church. Some women seem to be more in love with the idea of being married than they are with knowing Jesus Himself! Marriage is wonderful, but only in the context of fulfilling the will of God. You treat your husband the way the Church is to treat Christ every day for the rest of your life!

If you're still single, remember that your home-life alone with the Lord is still your proving ground for success. God may use your job or your ministry to expose issues He wants to deal with before you get married. This is an incredibly high calling for both men and women, and it is at the heart of being a Kingmaker. Serving an impersonal boss and keeping Christ-like character can be great preparation for serving a husband who loves you as Jesus loves the Church!

One of the single women in the Bible who received special recognition was Anna the prophetess, a widow who lived in the temple. At the time that Mary and Joseph took the baby Jesus to present Him to God, she was in position to recognize who He was and praise God aloud for His calling.

Biblical Kingmakers

Anna, the Prophetess

Single and serving God with fasting and prayers night and day, she was one of the first to see Jesus.

"Anna, a prophet, was also there in the Temple. She was the daughter of Phanuel from the tribe of Asher, and she was very old. Her husband died when they had been married only seven years. Then she lived as a widow to the age of eighty-four. She never left the Temple but stayed there day and night, worshiping God with fasting and prayer. She came along just as Simeon was talking with Mary and Joseph, and she began praising God. She talked about the child to everyone who had been waiting expectantly for God to rescue Jerusalem."[37]

Women like Anna enjoy being single because they can fully dedicate themselves to God. Single women who are uncomfortable with the constraints that come with being a wife and mother should consider whether or not they have been given the gift of celibacy, a gift that Paul rejoiced in (1 Corinthians 7:7). The joys that come with serving others are a byproduct of your fulfillment of God's plan for your life. God purposes to bless His single and married daughters in their personal and professional lives. You can find joy and contentment in that reality, even if you're single.

Making Jesus King in the earth has practical application to a single woman's everyday life. A Kingmaker, really, is simply someone who is willing to humble himself or herself to help someone else fulfill his or her destiny, and that is the call of every Christian.

Maybe you are called to be celibate for a long time, maybe even for life. Still, you will encounter many women who are married and may complain to you about their husbands. The principles in this book will help you understand what they are going through and how to help them obtain victory God's way.

---

[37] Luke 2:36-38 NLT.

SUBMITTING TO A PASTOR

Do you want to be promoted on the job or in the church? If you fight against submission to others, if you always have to be right and in control, God says, you can't be my kind of leader. You might be articulate; you might be educated; you might have a good mind. You might even be in a position of authority, but you're not God's leader. You're dealing with people from the position of your human weakness. God says you have to become a slave so that I can deal with your spirit. You become subject so that I can promote you.

This is also true of God's Woman, the Church. Instead of submitting to their pastor, let alone God, many churchgoers in our day are rebels who are always moving around from church to church. As soon as they get a little pressure from the pastor or feel uncomfortable, they don't consider it the moving of the Holy Ghost to bring them to repentance. They want to get out from under that discomfort and move on. They refuse to submit, even though that would be the best thing for them in terms of character development. That is not promotable. That is not a model of the Church's relationship to Christ.

People have a tendency to move until they find their comfort zone, but they won't ever find one if they stay in rebellion. They will carry those bad attitudes into every new church they join. You can fake it for a while in church just as you can fake it in marriage, but when somebody tells you to do something you don't like, the "True You" comes out. Then God can show you where you really are. You're not a worm, like Jesus. You're a snake who strikes back.

EMPOWERING OTHERS TO CHANGE

When you're a Kingmaker, you see everyone for where they are, and yet you see what God has ordained them to be. You treat them according to where they are going to be and not for where they are now. You low-look them. You say, like Sarah, "Yes, I will go in there and I will do what you say concerning Pharaoh. You're in charge."

I don't know what kind of man your husband is, or if you're married at all. I don't know anything about your church or career.

What I do know is that if you embrace the Kingmaker message of this book, you can become an unstoppable force for godly change in your household, your church, and your generation.

KINGMAKER CONFESSIONS
Speaking Boldly About Yourself
"David encouraged himself in the LORD his God."[38]

- As I submit my will in line with God's will, His favor increases in my life. I'm flowing in God's divine favor.
- God's favor changes my mentality. Even when I don't understand why I should submit, I give my thoughts and emotions to God, and He blesses me because I obey Him.
- Because I live for others, Christ-like meekness has come alive inside of me. God can reach me, and He can teach me. He can trust me with His secrets.
- I have the mind of Christ. My thoughts are the same as His thoughts. I enjoy thinking about how I can serve others.
- I'm blessed because God gives me a quiet spirit when I am helping others and they seem to take advantage of me. I'm never out of His control.
- I'm fulfilled by serving others for the sake of obedience to a principle of God, whether it seems right or not. I'm walking in real faith, and I am blessed!

KINGMAKER ACTIONS
Blessed By Doing His Will
". . . a doer of the work will be blessed."[39]

- Make a list of ways that you can show favor to someone to whom you are submitted. Take action on these points and then check them off.
- List reasons you don't submit to someone in authority whom you disrespect. What would Jesus do in your situation?

---

[38] 1 Samuel 30:6 KJV.
[39] James 1:25 NKJV.

- Pray about how you can win that person over by your attitude of submission. Remember, this road of reconciliation may be a rocky one, but it's taking you somewhere—closer to Christ-likeness.

KINGMAKER PRAYER
Submitting It All To God
". . . not my will, but thine, be done."[40]

When you pray, turn your faith toward God as your Father. You don't need faith toward your needs, but toward God. A child expects to receive from her father. Don't look to God for *things*. Look to God for God *Himself*, and, as Jesus said, all those things shall be added to you.[41] Delight yourself in the Lord. When you delight in Him, He says He'll give you the desires of your heart.[42]

Father, in Jesus' name I thank You that You have called me into liberty, but it's not a liberty to be separated from You. It's a liberty to be submitted to You and to try new things because I know that You are with me. Thank You for giving me the freedom to make decisions for myself, and then being there for me when I find out whether I missed it or got it right. Thank You that You're teaching me to be obedient in my heart so that I'll make more right decisions in my relationship with You and my relationships with others, without ever having to ask. Help me to have the same attitude toward others that Jesus has. Help me to be there for people when they are not at the level, and bring them to the level through my obedience to You and my selfless service to them. In Jesus' name I pray. Amen.

---

[40] Luke 22:42 KJV.
[41] See Matthew 6:33.
[42] See Psalm 37:4.

Chapter 5
Rewards Beyond This World

"Work from the heart for your real Master, for God, confident
that you'll get paid in full when you come into your inheritance.
Keep in mind always that the ultimate
Master you're serving is Christ."[1]

Think about the greatest material blessings you could ever
have on earth. Unlimited bank accounts. Mansions. Exotic cars.
Your own airplane. A Paris wardrobe. The greatest things you could
ever get are still, at best, things of this earth. They won't last. They
have to be fixed up, repaired, replaced. But everything you've
committed to God as a Kingmaker gives you treasures in this world
and the next because you're an heir, a joint-heir with Jesus, the Heir
of all things!

With Jesus, **we are heirs** **of all things**	*"God, who at various times and in various ways* *spoke in time past to the fathers by the prophets,* *has in these last days spoken to us by His Son,* *whom He has appointed heir of all things,* *through whom also He made the worlds."[2]*

THERE'S A GOOD REPORT OUT ABOUT YOU

When you know Jesus and you act like Jesus toward others in
your role as a Kingmaker, God rewards that. The Bible says in the
Scripture from Colossians 3 quoted above that "you'll get paid in
full when you come into your inheritance" because "the ultimate
Master you're serving is Christ."

---

[1] Colossians 3, *The Message.*
[2] Hebrews 1:1-3 NKJV.

Jesus is calling you to see things from a perspective other than earth.

You're on a journey of absolute commitment to the ways of God where God gives you rewards and an understanding of eternity. Hebrews 11 describes the faith of those who have gone before us who saw another country, a heavenly one. They didn't live just for today and they didn't see themselves as bound to what they saw on earth. They lived in a heavenly country—another realm of faith.

In this world, but citizens of an eternal realm	*"These all died in faith, not having received the promises, but having seen them afar off were assured of them, embraced them and confessed that they were strangers and pilgrims on the earth."*[3]

The Bible says, "Now faith is the substance of things hoped for, the evidence of things not seen."[4] What you say, what you think, and what you do in this world is enriched by how much you can see by faith of the eternal realm. God has a vision for your life that is much higher than the trials you are going through. When you get discouraged, He never loses His vision for you, because you represent the Church, and He has already called the Church "glorious." You are on the winning side.

When you follow the Lord, you're obedient to God, and you walk in the faith of God, then God can show you off. Your life becomes living evidence to others that He is real and the unseen world is a real world. Your faith-filled life gives evidence of His reality because you are living at a level that other people can't touch. You are more dedicated, more giving, more joyful than anyone they know. You are a believer who walks in His ways. God gives witness through you that His ways are good and true.

God approved of Abraham's life. He approved of Isaiah's life. He approved of Elijah's life. He approved of David's life. By what standard? By their faith—not by faith as in doctrine, but faith

---

[3] Hebrews 11:13 NKJV.
[4] Hebrews 11:1 KJV.

as in commitment. They believed and acted on their beliefs.

When you look back at Moses' life you can see his example as a spiritual father. In the same way, if Jesus tarries, the next generation will look back and see your life as an example of a Kingmaker who functioned beyond the level of this world. God can give you a good report. You are ordained for nothing less. You are called to have a good report in Heaven and in Earth.

All of the elders of the past are depending on us to fulfill the vision that they saw of a better world. God has released the Holy Spirit to us and the integrity of His name and His Word are actually coming to pass in the earth through us. Once you are determined that the will of the Lord must come to pass in your life, every enemy of God will be defeated. Every enemy of your soul will have to bow.

Your Faith Is Seen in Your Works

The Bible says that by faith Enoch was translated so that he would not see death.[5] Enoch was so committed to the Lord and to the things of God that death could not get a hold on his life. By faith he transcended the boundaries of the physical make-up of his body.

Even the earth's gravitational pull couldn't keep him here. He dematerialized. The Bible says by his faith—by his commitment—he was translated. It says in that same verse that he had this testimony, that he pleased God. He was so pleasing to God that God couldn't keep him here on this earth, because the man had gone ahead of the test schedule of God. He moved in the dimension that he was better suited for. He lived in the dimension of God so fully that he could not even stay on the earth.

He pleased God | *"By faith Enoch was translated that he should not see death; and was not found, because God had translated him: for before his translation he had this testimony, that he pleased God."[6]*

Doesn't that level of faith—being translated instead of dying—seem like a goal greater than believing God for a car or a

---

[5] See Hebrews 11:5.
[6] Hebrews 11:5 KJV.

new job? In God's eternal realm, you can believe God for a
transformation in yourself and those you serve as a Kingmaker who
is off the charts. O ye of little faith! God, help us with our unbelief!

Witnesses from Heaven Are Cheering You On

In Hebrews 12:1 (KJV) the Bible says, "Wherefore seeing we are
compassed about with so great a cloud of witnesses." The witnesses
are the people the Bible talks about in Hebrews 11 who died in faith.
They are with God now, witnesses looking over the portals of
Heaven who see the destiny of God made manifest in the Church
here on earth.

Surrounded by cheering witnesses, we keep our eyes on Jesus	*"Therefore, since we are surrounded by such a huge crowd of witnesses to the life of faith, let us strip off every weight that slows us down, especially the sin that so easily trips us up. And let us run with endurance the race God has set before us. We do this by keeping our eyes on Jesus."[7]*

What are they seeing in your life beyond what they obtained in
theirs? When you have their level of commitment, you will have the
same fruit that they had. You can go beyond them with a sacrificial
life beyond the level of theirs. That is what they are hoping for. They
are cheering us on from a place of eternal life. They want us to
exceed them!

We sow to the Spirit to reap life everlasting	*"Those who live only to satisfy their own sinful nature will harvest decay and death from that sinful nature. But those who live to please the Spirit will harvest everlasting life from the Spirit. So let's not get tired of doing what is good. At just the right time we will reap a harvest of blessing if we don't give up."[8]*

---

[7] Hebrews 12:1-2 NLT.
[8] Galatians 6:8-9 NLT.

We don't grow faint in our commitment when the people we are trying to make into kings don't cooperate with us or we fall short, because God has a greater vision for us. Our *potential* is unlimited.

Say that out loud: My potential is unlimited!
"Let us lay aside every weight and the sin which doth
so easily beset us, and let us run with patience the
race that is set before us."[9]

Faith is belief and it is also commitment. Your commitment is the substance of things hoped for. When you are a Kingmaker, you hope for others' greatness. You have faith for it. You have the commitment to make it happen. You are willing to prioritize your life according to the same things that God has as His priorities.

The God Kind of Commitment

When you set God's goals as a priority in your life, you receive power. His goal is for you to grow and help others to grow. When the things you hope for are in line with the things that God hopes for, and when you have the same vision God has for someone you are making into a king, that fuels the fire of your dedication. God created you with the potential for the same passion that Jesus has for helping people fulfill their destiny. Line up your thought life with His thought life. Line up your deeds with His priorities. That is the purpose of faith. That is the purpose of commitment.

FOCUS ON INNER ATTRIBUTES

When you are a Kingmaker, you change your focus from externals to "the hidden man of the heart, in that which is not corruptible, even the ornament of a meek and a quiet spirit."[10]

Meekness and a quiet spirit are inward qualities that people can see outwardly. They are jewels. When the Bible says "whose adorning" it's talking about what people see on the outside. Make sure that what comes out of you isn't you but what comes out of you

---

[9] Hebrews 12:1 KJV.
[10] 1 Peter 3:4 KJV.

is God, "which in the sight of God is of great price." Don't be distracted. Do that which is of value to God. Being in subjection is an opportunity to increase in value before God.

In 1 Corinthians 3 the Bible says that our lives show gold, silver, and precious stones, but they also show wood, hay and stubble. Your works will be tested by fire to see what sort they are.

We are building for rewards through works that can withstand fire

"Now anyone who builds on that foundation may use gold, silver, jewels, wood, hay, or straw. But there is going to come a time of testing at the judgment day to see what kind of work each builder has done. Everyone's work will be put through the fire to see whether or not it keeps its value. If the work survives the fire, that builder will receive a reward. But if the work is burned up, the builder will suffer great loss. The builders themselves will be saved, but like someone escaping through a wall of flames."[11]

Your ultimate work as a Kingmaker is in pressing past your flesh into the face of Jesus and seeing His heart. When you bring your experience of salvation into a real walk with God, there is no doubt that what you're thinking is what God is thinking. What you're speaking is what God is speaking. Your goals are the same as what God has determined for the generation. Just like Jesus, you are willing to lay down your life and live for others.

KINGMAKER CONFESSIONS
Speaking Boldly About Yourself
"David encouraged himself in the LORD his God."[12]

- I will find more of Jesus because I am going after Him with a new intensity.

---

[11] 1 Corinthians 3:12-15 NLT.
[12] 1 Samuel 30:6 KJV.

- I can become like Jesus because I am seeking Him with all my heart.
- The next generation can gain from my example as a Kingmaker who functions beyond the level of this world. I am ordained for nothing less.
- I am called to have a good report before God and before the witnesses in Heaven and Earth.
- I will receive rewards in the next world because I am following Jesus, and I am a joint-heir with Jesus, and Jesus is Heir of all things.
- I will focus on developing Christ-likeness in myself in "the hidden man of the heart."

KINGMAKER ACTIONS
Blessed By Doing His Will
". . . a doer of the work will be blessed."[13]

- Do the right things and confirmation will follow. What right things can you do now that will affect your place in eternity? Make a list.
- It says in Hebrews 11:4, "By faith Abel offered unto God a more excellent sacrifice than Cain, by which he obtained witness that he was righteous." Abel didn't get the witness before he did the right thing, but after it. Do something and then look for the witness. Seek the face of the Lord.
- The Lord is calling you to see into another world. How do you envision the "new you" who will be developing in the future? List your attributes.

KINGMAKER PRAYER
Submitting It All To God
". . . not my will, but thine, be done."[14]

When was the last time you laid down prostrate at the altars of God's presence? There is something about this generation that we hardly pray on our knees, let alone our faces. It's as though God isn't

---

[13] James 1:25 NKJV.
[14] Luke 22:42 KJV.

really there. In many cases even in our prayers we pray as though He were distant from us. I look at myself sometimes and say, "Boone, you're religious. You are hollering as though God has ear problems or something. As if He has a deaf spirit." Then I am looking up in the air as if He is way off somewhere. Do you know why? Because at that moment He does seem far off to me. I am more into religion than the fact that God is actually here with me. What you and I need is an understanding of the reality of God Himself, personally. The Lord is with us!

Father, in Jesus' name, let the glory of God come upon me now. May the sense of the presence of the Lord be with me both inside and outside. May the angelic hosts reveal themselves to me by God's permission. May I rise up above the self-life now. May I be a mighty woman of God. May I feel a divine sense of the presence of the Lord. May I go into the Word of the Lord and may the Word of God become my life and lead me into righteous paths. May my weaknesses be overcome by the presence of the Lord and may the blood of the Lord bring forgiveness for my sins. May I have a vision to become an elder, a mother to the motherless. Make my life an example that people can see. May the light of the Lord rise up inside of me so that people can see that Jesus is real because they can see Jesus in me. In Jesus' name I pray. Amen.

SECTION 2

Serving as
a Kingmaker

Chapter 6
Kingmaker Wives

". . . and let the wife see that she respects and reverences her husband [that she notices him, regards him, honors him, prefers him, venerates, and esteems him; and that she defers to him, praises him, and loves and admires him exceedingly]."[1]

What makes the Christmas movie *It's a Wonderful Life* with Jimmy Stewart one of America's all-time favorites? It's not only the self-sacrifice and community spirit of the main character, George Bailey. It's also how the film portrays the way his Kingmaker wife, Mary (played by Donna Reed), esteems him, and loves and admires him exceedingly!

Take the rain-soaked scene in Bert's taxicab as George, flushed with excitement on his wedding day, flashes the stack of bills that he has been saving up for their honeymoon. Suddenly, he notices something strange. Mobs of people are crowded around the door of his family's Building and Loan company. It's the middle of the day, but the doors are locked, and the customers can't get in. It's a run on the bank!

George leaps out of the taxicab, ignoring the pleas of his new wife, and runs to open the doors. With agitated customers pressed against him, he forces his way inside and finds frowsy Uncle Billy in a panic, gulping a swig of alcohol as he says distractedly, "This is a pickle, George. This is a pickle."

Apparently the film's villain, Mr. Potter, the banker, has called in an outstanding loan and Uncle Billy has taken all of the small firm's cash to pay him off. When Mr. Potter puts out the word that the people's money is gone, they panic. Shortly after George arrives, Mary comes on the scene, and that Kingmaker wife saves

---

[1] Ephesians 5:33 AMP.

the day! She says to the crowd, "Do you need money? Here!" And she holds up their entire savings of $2,000 that they had set aside for their honeymoon and their new life.

That Mary was something else. She loved George as she loved herself. She still had more surprises to come. While her new husband was using all of their nest egg to rescue the Building and Loan by giving all depositors at least a few dollars on their accounts to tide them over, she went out and carried out a plan. She decided to bless her new husband even more, even though he had almost forgotten her in the rush of the moment.

Mary enlisted friend Bert and some other guys to fix up a broken-down house in the neighborhood that was so bad George and Mary in an impetuous moment of their courtship had once thrown rocks through the windows. Now it was going to be home. Mary tacked up travel posters and placed rain buckets under the leaks. She even lit a fire in the fireplace and persuaded the guys to sing a serenade outside the window as soon as George arrived. That woman knew how to be a Kingmaker. She never complained about the lost honeymoon, not to mention the money! She found her fulfillment in fulfilling destiny with her husband.

Fulfilling Heaven's Destiny with Your Husband

A husband and wife are made to fulfill the purposes of God together. When a Kingmaker wife loves her husband, that represents the way the Church loves Christ. What really makes a house a home? Beyond externals and frills, what makes us want to be at home more than anywhere else? Having a home where love is, just like Heaven.

Heaven on Earth	*"That your days may be multiplied, and the days of your children, in the land which the LORD sware unto your fathers to give them, as the days of heaven upon the earth."[2]*

As a Kingmaker, you can be a Mary Bailey. You can make *any* home into a place that is just like Heaven. You don't need a

---

[2] Deuteronomy 11:21 KJV.

20,000 square-foot mansion or the finest furniture, because *you* create the environment that represents God's Kingdom—a place of giving, forgiving, and love.

Life filled with love for others	*"Live a life filled with love for others, following the example of Christ, who loved you and gave himself as a sacrifice to take away your sins. And God was pleased, because that sacrifice was like sweet perfume to him."*[3]

SOMEONE HE WANTS TO COME HOME TO

I travel a lot in my ministry. In the process, I eat at nice restaurants and stay at first class hotels all over the world. My wife and I have been blessed to take vacations in foreign countries and cruises in exotic places. But when I come right down to it, there's no place like home. Most days, I would rather enjoy a quiet evening at home than be anywhere else. That's saying a lot, since I always have a steady flow of guests, adult offspring and ministry people living with me!

How does a home become a "no place like home" place? By what you do! You make the environment of your home that way! You (and your husband) cultivate an atmosphere in your home that makes it an attraction to others. It smells good in your house because it's filled with loving, giving people.

If your husband is never home, maybe there are good reasons for that. Maybe he works long hours or holds two jobs. Maybe he's in ministry or he's a physician, and people in need are pulling on him all day long. Maybe your husband has no control over his schedule, but in other cases maybe he does. Maybe he's one of those guys (and they know who they are) who would rather hang out with the boys than be at home with his wife. He doesn't rush home from work. He takes his time. He'd rather eat in the car than sit at the table with his family. He's looking for excuses to stay out.

---

[3] Ephesians 5:2 NLT.

First, let me say that the bottom line for husbands is that no man has a right to make excuses not to go home. It's an abomination that any man would neglect his family like that. Even if the house is a wreck, the kids are all sick and his wife hasn't showered or done her hair all day long, he should still rush to get home because that's his family we're talking about, and he's supposed to be like Christ is to the Church. These are the people who put him first in their lives.

However, if you are a wife, you can take it as a personal challenge to create an atmosphere in your home that is so awesome that the brother can't wait to get home. The way you treat him from the moment he walks in the door is so off the charts that he forgets all his other options! You're unbeatable!

When a husband rushes home because he's eager to be with the wife he loves, it's like these lines from the Song of Solomon:

Your husband loves to see your face and hear your voice	*"O my dove, in the clefts of the rock, In the secret places of the cliff, Let me see your face, Let me hear your voice; For your voice is sweet, And your face is lovely."*[4]

Love Him by Listening to His Day

You can force your husband to come home because he knows that if he doesn't he'll get fussed at, but that won't give him a heart for you. Become that lovely woman in the Song of Solomon. Speak in that musical voice he loves. The brother has been out there all day long on the job. People have been hassling him, working him over. Maybe his employees are shirking off, not working as they should. People are criticizing him. If the marketplace is like that, when he comes home and says he had a rough day, what does he hear from his wife? "My day was worse than yours!" It might be true, but marriage is not a competition for who can have the biggest pity party! It's a team effort, and sometimes you need to listen and meet his needs without complaining about yours.

---

[4] Song of Solomon 2:14 NKJV.

| *Interested in the other person's needs* | *"Don't think only about your own affairs, but be interested in others, too, and what they are doing."[5]* |

You say, "I'm so happy to see you! Sit down here; take your shoes off." You start loving on him. You've already got the kids taken care of and they know that this is Daddy and Momma's time. Maybe you've been at work too, but you still have dinner on the table smelling great.

What's happening to him? Even if he's treated like a nobody on the job, when he comes in the house his wife treats him like a king! With your self-sacrifice you're making another human being into a king! Selfishness has no reward. It's an empty cistern that is never filled. A home environment that a guy wants to come home to is the kind that a Kingmaker creates. That gives him something to brag about to his friends.

| *Clean and innocent with your light shining* | *"In everything you do, stay away from complaining and arguing, so that no one can speak a word of blame against you. You are to live clean, innocent lives as children of God in a dark world full of crooked and perverse people. Let your lives shine brightly before them."[6]* |

You're *His* Woman

Feminists might tell you that doing nice things to serve a man is beneath you. You shouldn't have to do that stuff just because you're a woman. Well, you don't *have* to do anything. No one can force you to be nice to your husband when you don't want to do it. No one can make you submit, just as no one can make you become a Christian! You're not serving him because you're a woman. You're serving him because you're *his* woman! You're a Kingmaker!

---

[5] Philippians 2:4 NLT.
[6] Philippians 2:14-16 NLT.

You understand the relationship of the Church to Christ, so you voluntarily subject yourself to acts of King-making—whether toward Jesus or your husband.

How are you going to help your husband reach his potential? By criticizing him? Or by doing what Jesus does with us: *treating him according to what he can be, not what he deserves.* By reminding him that you know more or earn more? *Or by blessing him with your words.*

The blessings of God are on you when you love somebody who doesn't have a clue, who still struggles with that manly pride and ego. Your extravagant love makes your home like Heaven when he knows he doesn't deserve it. The brother knows that he needs to get himself together, but you're making him into a king. That blows him away. You might have just as much education as he has. You might make more money in the marketplace, or if you're home you could make more money if you went out and worked. But the brother knows you love him just the same. That builds him up! That wakes him up! That's the way to love him.

WAYS TO KEEP HIM RUSHING HOME

Here are some practical ways to make your husband want to keep rushing home.

1. Greet him with a look that says, "I love you."
2. Fix dinner.
3. Allow him time to unwind if he needs it.
4. Surprise him often as soon as he arrives.
5. Make jokes about your bad days.
6. Keep your home neat and clean.
7. Give your family space to let down and relax.

1. Greet him with a look that says, "I love you." Even if it's been a terrible day and you're right in the middle of something when he walks in the door, try to put that aside for a minute and focus on him. Hang up the phone. Look him in the eyes. Smile in that intimate way that says, "I'm yours alone." Saying something loving to your husband when he walks in the door makes you look so gorgeous that he forgets about his day and is so happy that he can finally be with you.

Ravished by one look of your eyes

"You have ravished my heart,
My sister, my spouse;
You have ravished my heart
With one look of your eyes,
With one link of your necklace.
How fair is your love,
My sister, my spouse!
How much better than wine is your love."[7]

2. Fix dinner. Remember that old adage that the way to a man's heart is through his stomach? Good food is a great motivator. If you can't cook and don't want to learn, how about picking up something on the way home? Don't always force him to go out because that's what *you* want to do. Find a way to make your meal intimate—at home with your husband. Set a beautiful table with candles, flowers, tablecloth, etc. Treat him like a king.

3. Allow him time to unwind if he needs it. He may come home ready to talk, or he may want to relax and think for a minute. Try to give him space to do either.

4. Surprise him often as soon as he arrives. Don't forget to keep him guessing. Maybe it's a gift, a favorite dessert, or something that you helped the kids to paint and paste and put Daddy's name on it. All of those things add up to the feeling that home is where he's cared for, valued, and appreciated.

5. Make jokes about your bad days. There's an old saying, "If life gives you lemons, make lemonade." Instead of dragging your husband down with a list of your day's trials, laugh about it and say things to make him laugh, too.

---

[7] Song of Solomon 4:9-10 NKJV.

A merry heart	*" . . . he that is of a merry heart hath a continual feast. "[8]*

6. Keep your home neat and clean. Some men don't care a lot about neatness but some do. At a minimum keep the home presentable, unless there's a last-minute disaster. Teach your children to pick up after themselves. Have scented candles and a fire in the fireplace, and add other things to create an inviting atmosphere at home. Clutter makes everybody feel worse, so keep out the clutter. Help a messy brother out.

I remind men that the Bible doesn't say that a wife has to do all the housework. "Thy wife shalt iron" isn't one of the Ten Commandments! I actually do the ironing in my house. Still, if you want your home to be orderly and inviting, keep it clean. You can move beyond the thinking that says cleaning is drudgery and you don't have to do it. If you can afford it, hire a housekeeper and let her enjoy it for you.

So much of your attitude toward housework is determined by how you look at it. Scrubbing and mopping isn't glamorous, but you *can* get a revelation for it if you don't complain! When your motivation comes from Heaven, your work and your attitude will make you feel like a saint. There's nothing in the Bible that says you have to do it all yourself. Even the Proverbs 31 woman had handmaidens.

7. Give your family space to let down and relax. When you are a Kingmaker, your home is a place where everyone can be themselves. You keep it clean, but you don't focus on cleaning so much that you won't let anybody mess it up.

CONQUERING NEEDS-CONSCIOUSNESS

Practical principles are important and helpful, but for real Christians, *they cannot replace the foundational reality that marriage represents the spiritual relationship between Christ and*

---

[8] Proverbs 15:15 KJV.

the Church. When you know Him, He meets your needs a lot better than any mate.

God meets your needs	*"But my God shall supply all your need according to his riches in glory by Christ Jesus."*[9]

Somebody might try to tell you that spiritual people are no good at marriage, because marriage is more practical than spiritual. That marriage is about meeting needs—sex, money, and a clean and fashionable house. The wife keeps herself thin and the husband is always getting promoted. Many of the marriage books you find even in Christian bookstores deal mainly with needs in the soul realm: better communication, learning about one another's unique personalities, and so on. However, we also need to keep talking about Christ and the Church in every marriage relationship.

As you live out the truths of the Kingdom of God in your marriage, you move past living at the level of needs. You are no longer in bondage to your inner conflicts about gender, a dysfunctional background, self-pity, or anything else. You are a mature adult woman who has moved forward to fulfill the will of God. You have the ability inside of you to come up to the level where you fulfill God's purposes and achieve real significance.

Don't focus on the natural realm. When you focus on the natural, some human has to meet your needs, because you're thinking about what you don't have instead of realizing that you're the carrier of the substance that can fulfill the earth.

---

[9] Philippians 4:19 KJV.

*Needs-
consciousness
comes from
the devil!*

*"The serpent was the shrewdest of all
the wild animals the Lord God had made. One
day he asked the woman, 'Did God really say
you must not eat the fruit from any of the trees
in the garden?'*

*" 'Of course we may eat fruit from the
trees in the garden,' the woman replied. 'It's
only the fruit from the tree in the middle of the
garden that we are not allowed to eat. God
said, "You must not eat it or even touch it; if
you do, you will die." '*

*" 'You won't die!' the serpent replied to
the woman. 'God knows that your eyes will be
opened as soon as you eat it, and you will be
like God, knowing both good and evil.'*

*"The woman was convinced. She saw
that the tree was beautiful and its fruit looked
delicious, and she wanted the wisdom it would
give her. So she took some of the fruit and ate
it. Then she gave some to her husband, who
was with her, and he ate it, too. At that moment
their eyes were opened, and they suddenly felt
shame at their nakedness. So they sewed fig
leaves together to cover themselves."*[10]

Focus on the spiritual realm. When you focus on the
spiritual realm, you have no needs, because in God all your needs are
supplied. A consciousness of needs didn't come from God. It came
from the devil. He convinced the woman that there was something
else that God had not given her in the natural realm of the Garden.
Therefore, she should bypass God's instructions and make up her
own rules for life. That didn't work then, and it doesn't work now.
As my Momma always said, "The Devil is a liar!" God *can* supply
all your needs!

---

[10] Genesis 3:1-7 NLT.

Think about how many times you have heard people discount God's ability to meet their needs and try to rely on their own logic. That's how the man and woman got kicked out of the Garden and lost that perfect peace. Go after what you need by being obedient to God.

If the Devil couldn't keep you from being saved, he tries to keep you living below the standard of your call. He tries to blind you so that you think of your natural needs and inadequacies—what you don't have—rather than the reality of who you are in Christ.

He gets you focused on your lack of education, your disqualifications, your unworthiness, your limitations because you've done such and such in the past.

At all times you are dealing with that which is forever vs. that which is temporary. Your life will be changed as you look beyond your needs and failures and into the glorious future that you can see in the face of God. That is forever.

SECRETS OF TRUE INTIMACY

What makes a house beautiful to your family on the inside? It's intimacy.

Your home looks beautiful because it's a secret sanctuary where your family can be alone together in their own little world and loving it.

It's the world where you and your husband are in charge, and it's the best there is.

It's not a public magazine spread. It's a private garden of a family's love.

You're a priest caring for the sanctuary of God!

The secret place of intimacy and commitment

"You are like a private garden, my treasure, my bride! You are like a spring that no one else can drink from, a fountain of my own. You are like a lovely orchard bearing precious fruit, with the rarest of perfumes: nard and saffron, calamus and cinnamon, myrrh and aloes, perfume from every incense tree, and every other lovely spice. You are a garden fountain, a well of living water, as refreshing as the streams from the Lebanon mountains."[11]

When God created Adam and his wife, they were naked and not ashamed.[12] They were vulnerable; they hid nothing from each other and flowed in perfect intimacy. After the Fall, Adam and Eve put on fig leaves to cover themselves and hide from God. The fear of rejection and exposure entered human relationships. Those fig leaves were dying. That covering was useless. Man can never create an adequate covering for his shortcomings. They are bound to come out eventually, especially in marriage.

Every one of us is naked to the Almighty just like a baby coming out of the womb. God wants us to live out that kind of authenticity in our marriages, and many times He needs the wife to go first! If you win your husband by your external sexuality, you have to keep it up, and you never know when he will find somebody else who can satisfy his lusts more than you do. However, if you win your husband on the basis of spiritual intimacy and Christ-like love, that love never ends. That's the kind of marriage God sees for you and for His Son when He marries the Bride.

True intimacy is a matter of cultivating the presence of God in your life until you can be naked and unashamed with God and your husband in every area of your life. You have no secret sins. You have no hidden motives. You don't try to manipulate him. You keep it real. In the presence of God you can break down and admit

---

[11] Song 4:12-15 NLT.
[12] See Genesis 2:25.

who you really are. You're not trying to say everything properly; you're not trying to be something that you're not. You just realize that God is there and you strip yourself of artificiality and give Him His due.

If I can be vulnerable and intimate with God, I can be that way with my wife. I'm not against buying my wife beautiful lingerie for the marriage bed, but if that's all we have going on, we haven't got anything going on. You can initiate things that bring more intimacy with your husband by looking beautiful AND by being more intimate with him because of Christ! Intimacy in marriage is genuine Christianity at its best. It's real! When you're real, you're on your way to a fulfilled marriage.

INWARD STEPS TO INTIMACY

Below are eight personal goals for a new beginning that will help you to create an environment of intimacy in your marriage by taking steps toward your personal inner change.

1. Be a person of prayer and intimacy with God.
2. Cultivate inner beauty.
3. Focus on Jesus' acceptance of you, not your husband's acceptance.
4. Pray together.
5. Read the Bible aloud with your husband.
6. Don't reject your husband when he hurts or displeases you.
7. Win his heart with your virtue, loyalty, and unselfish love.
8. Keep a "good forgetter" when he wrongs you.

1. Be a person of prayer and intimacy with God, praying for your husband, forgiving him, and living a dedicated Christian life before God and your husband.

| *Value of a virtuous woman* | *"Who can find a virtuous woman? for her price is far above rubies. The heart of her husband doth safely trust in her."[13]* |

2. Cultivate inner beauty.

Most women put on jewelry from the outside, but God says, "I'm going to put some priceless jewelry on you that will grow from the inside—the hidden man of the heart." This jewelry makes you more beautiful than any jewelry you can buy. It's incorruptible jewelry. It looks good to God and your husband. Keep your inner beauty intact for his sake and for the cause of Christ.

| *Inner beauty of a godly woman* | *"Do not let your adornment be merely outward—arranging the hair, wearing gold, or putting on fine apparel—rather let it be the hidden person of the heart, with the incorruptible beauty of a gentle and quiet spirit, which is very precious in the sight of God."[14]* |

3. Focus on Jesus' acceptance of you, not your husband's acceptance.

What causes a woman to turn against her husband? She doesn't want to be put down. She wants to be appreciated. She wants to be accepted. Jesus can help you out. He says you should focus on *His* acceptance so that you can grow in the ornaments and the jewelry of the inner life that He brings out in you, and then you won't need so much reinforcement from your husband. If your husband is backslidden or rebellious and seems almost hostile to you, then maybe the best you can do is to just serve him and submit to him as you would to the Lord, but don't blow up or give up. The brother needs you.

4. Pray together.

Your own intimacy with the Father will be proven in intimate prayer together. Prayer often marks the difference between a focus on heart intimacy that builds your house on a rock and a focus on sexual intimacy that builds your house on sand.

---

[13] Mark 14:38 NKJV.
[14] 1 Peter 3:2-5 NKJV.

If two of you shall agree, it shall be done, for I am there	*"Again I say unto you, That if two of you shall agree on earth as touching any thing that they shall ask, it shall be done for them of my Father which is in heaven. For where two or three are gathered together in my name, there am I in the midst of them."*[15]

5. Read the Bible aloud with your husband. Stay on the same page with your husband by reading the same Book—the Bible.

Words to build a life on	*"These words I speak to you are not incidental additions to your life, homeowner improvements to your standard of living. They are foundational words, words to build a life on. If you work these words into your life, you are like a smart carpenter who built his house on solid rock. Rain poured down, the river flooded, a tornado hit—but nothing moved that house. It was fixed to the rock. But if you just use my words in Bible studies and don't work them into your life, you are like a stupid carpenter who built his house on the sandy beach. When a storm rolled in and the waves came up, it collapsed like a house of cards."*[16]

6. Don't reject your husband when he hurts or displeases you. Never use rejection as a weapon. Don't reject your husband with the silent treatment, insulting words or withholding sex. Even if your husband is unkind, you respond with mercy and love. That's what Jesus did. He wants you to be like Him.

---

[15] Matthew 18:19-20 KJV.
[16] Matthew 7 *The Message*.

"But if you're treated badly for good behavior and continue in spite of it to be a good servant, that is what counts with God. This is the kind of life you've been invited into, the kind of life Christ lived. He suffered everything that came his way so you would know that it could be done, and also know how to do it, step-by-step.

"He never did one thing wrong, Not once said anything amiss.

Jesus suffered in silence

"They called him every name in the book and he said nothing back. He suffered in silence, content to let God set things right. He used his servant body to carry our sins to the Cross so we could be rid of sin, free to live the right way. His wounds became your healing. You were lost sheep with no idea who you were or where you were going. Now you're named and kept for good by the Shepherd of your souls."[17]

7. Win his heart with your virtue, loyalty, and unselfish love. In many ways, show him you love him by putting him first.

Love isn't 'me first'

"Love doesn't strut, Doesn't have a swelled head, Doesn't force itself on others, Isn't always "me first," Doesn't fly off the handle, Doesn't keep score of the sins of others, Doesn't revel when others grovel, Takes pleasure in the flowering of truth."[18]

---

[17] 1 Peter 2:20-25 *The Message.*
[18] 1 Corinthians 13:4-6 *The Message.*

8. Keep a "good forgetter" about how he has wronged you. God forgets our transgressions and puts them as far away from us as the east is from the west. And He says He doesn't remember our sins.

Forgive and forget, as God does	*"As far as the east is from the west, so far hath he removed our transgressions from us."[19]* *"I, even I, am he that blotteth out thy transgressions for mine own sake, and will not remember thy sins."[20]*

OUTWARD STEPS TO INTIMACY

Here are eight practical to a new beginning to encourage your husband to build more intimacy between the two of you, because he is captivated by your holy beauty.

Captivated by your holy beauty	*"Be good wives to your husbands, responsive to their needs. There are husbands who, indifferent as they are to any words about God, will be captivated by your life of holy beauty."[21]*

1. Share with him what you are hearing from God and let him judge it.
2. Give him what he likes because you're a giver by nature.
3. Ask his opinion on issues.
4. Read books together and grow together emotionally and intellectually.
5. Turn TV watching into a sharing time.
6. Plan regular date nights and vacations together.
7. Explain to him kindly how to show more love to you.
8. Give him opportunities to watch TV alone or with his buddies.

---

[19] Psalm 103:12 KJV.
[20] Isaiah 43:25 KJV.
[21] 1 Peter 3:1-2 *The Message.*

1. Share with him what you are hearing from God and let him judge it. Share thoughts with him that you feel the Lord is showing you. Ask him what he thinks about it. This gives him an opportunity to be your spiritual leader. Listen to what he says and take it seriously, even if you are the more "spiritual" one. He will never grow into headship if you don't give him room to give you his feedback. Don't let your spiritual pride hinder your husband's spiritual growth. Allow him to confirm what you think is a God said. That's a biblical principle you can build your married life on.

| ***Seek confirmation from your husband*** | *"In the mouth of two or three witnesses shall every word be established."*[22] |

2. Give him what he likes, because you're a giver by nature. Notice how he receives love the best. Does he like gifts or cards? Does he prefer candy or a back rub? What are his favorite foods? His favorite restaurants? How does he like to keep the environment of the home? Make him feel special by doing things regularly that say, "I love you. I want your life to be blessed by being with me."

| ***Give, and you will receive*** | *"If you give, you will receive. Your gift will return to you in full measure, pressed down, shaken together to make room for more, and running over. Whatever measure you use in giving--large or small--it will be used to measure what is given back to you."*[23] |

3. Ask his opinion on issues. Show your love for him by your respect for his opinions and insight. Ask him his opinions on things that interest him, such as politics, sports, finances, social issues, etc. Tell him where you stand, and ask for input. Don't dominate him with your opinions. Go low on him and hear him out, in love.

---

[22] 2 Corinthians 13:1 KJV.
[23] Luke 6:38 NLT.

If you don't love, you've gotten nowhere

"If I speak with human eloquence and angelic ecstasy but don't love, I'm nothing but the creaking of a rusty gate.

"If I speak God's Word with power, revealing all his mysteries and making everything plain as day, and if I have faith that says to a mountain, 'Jump,' and it jumps, but I don't love, I'm nothing.

"If I give everything I own to the poor and even go to the stake to be burned as a martyr, but I don't love, I've gotten nowhere. So, no matter what I say, what I believe, and what I do, I'm bankrupt without love."[24]

4. Read books together and grow together emotionally and intellectually. Read a book together and discuss it. Make the first book something that interests him.

5. Turn TV watching into a sharing time. When you watch TV together, carry on a conversation. If he wants to watch sports shows, don't talk all the time. Let him be content to have you beside him— not demanding attention, just in love.

Love that lasts

"Love never dies. Inspired speech will be over some day; praying in tongues will end; understanding will reach its limit. We know only a portion of the truth, and what we say about God is always incomplete. But when the Complete arrives, our incompletes will be canceled."[25]

6. Plan regular date nights and vacations together. This is actually his responsibility, but you can help.

---

[24] 1 Corinthians 13:1-3 *The Message.*
[25] 1 Corinthians 13:8-10 *The Message.*

Let's go away together	*"Come, my beloved,* *Let us go forth to the field;* *Let us lodge in the villages.* *Let us get up early to the vineyards;* *Let us see if the vine has budded,* *Whether the grape blossoms are open,* *And the pomegranates are in bloom.* *There I will give you my love."*[26]

7. Explain to him kindly how to show more love to you. If there is a way you would like him to show you love (gift, card, hug, etc.) ask him humbly. It will be hard for him to get defensive if you say: "Honey, it would make me so happy if you wrote me a card this week." Sometimes the brother really is clueless and needs help!

8. Give him opportunities to watch TV alone or with his buddies whether you think the program is worthwhile or not. Don't fuss if they make a mess. Honor him in front of his friends. Keep the big picture in mind—making your home like Heaven.

COULD YOU OBEY YOUR HUSBAND?

How do you become a beautiful wife? How do you adorn yourself? How do you become a wife of great price? How do you become qualified to oversee others outside the home? By submitting or being in subjection to your husband.

Trusting God by being in subjection	*"For after this manner in the old time the holy women also, who trusted in God, adorned themselves, being in subjection unto their own husbands."*[27]

---

[26] Song of Solomon 7:11-12 NKJV.
[27] 1 Peter 3:5 KJV.

Subjection is an attitude, and then it's an act. When you have the attitude of subjection—a slave's heart—then you can prove it out. Again, the Bible says that Sarah obeyed Abraham, calling him "Lord." Try calling your husband "Lord." We say that to Jesus, but we say it so quickly, and it's so trite. The Bible doesn't say that Abraham said to Sarah, "You are to call me Lord." His Kingmaker wife proved in obedience to him that he was her lord, and she was a servant under subjection to him. Can you see that?

Abraham said, "Go into Abimelech's harem, and tell him you're my sister." Abimelech was going to have sex with her. I'm going outside of the Bible in what I'm saying next, but it is just for the purpose of explanation. God had to come to Abimelech and say, "I'm going to kill you." Why? He was going to have sex with this woman Sarah. She didn't know what she would do, but she knew that her husband, whom she called Lord, said, "Go over there and tell him you're my sister."

Sarah's Vulnerability Because of Her Submission
By not telling the king that she was married to Abraham, Sarah became vulnerable to Abimelech. In Middle East thinking, Abraham knew exactly what he was doing. He said, "If I tell Abimelech that she is my wife, he will kill me and take her." She didn't just call him Lord. She acted it out. Why did she do it? She trusted God. How was that trust in God worked out? In obeying what her husband said.

Unafraid to say to him "Lord" | *". . . just as Sarah obeyed Abraham, calling him lord, and you have become her children if you do what is right without being frightened by any fear."*[28]

That verse says that we are all children of Abraham—all of us, male and female, "as long as ye do well." Notice the conditions laid down here: You are daughters of Abraham not just by having faith by doctrine. You are children of Abraham "as long as ye do

---

[28] 1 Peter 3:6 NASB.

well." You move out of the letter into the life. You walk in the spirit
of obedience by subjection—total dependency upon God.

You demonstrate your total trust in Him. If you get under
subjection to man because you trust in God, what does God call you?
A holy woman. No vile woman was going to Abimelech's harem.
She was a holy woman. She trusted in God through her husband.

Sarah didn't have a revelation of God. Her husband had the
revelation. God appeared to her husband and her husband told her
about it. She trusted in her husband. God says you're a holy woman
because you're in subjection to your own husband. He told her to do
things that were unthinkable, yet God was with her.

Many Christians have never heard of a life like that. What is
your challenge? Fear. You don't want to walk like that. Even if
potentially God could come to your defense in a supernatural way,
you don't want to risk it. You want to stay in control and keep your
husband out of control when it relates to your life.

How many wives not only want to call their husbands "Lord"
but also want their husbands to lord it over them? You have to go
back to your grandma and your great-grandma to know what it is to
be a holy woman like that. I remarked earlier about how they worked
at making their husbands lords. They starched clothes on a wash
board until their hands were almost raw. They didn't have the lotions
that we use. They used Vaseline to keep their hands half way decent.
Then when the man came home, they served him. They had his hot
meal all ready and his clothes clean. They had the house in shape.
They brought him whatever else he needed, fixed his bed, then got
up in the morning early to fix his breakfast and have it all ready
before he left. Those women said, "I'm not even worried about it.
My hands are to be used for work. I get a sense of fulfillment from
taking care of my husband."

In our generation we have gotten so far away from that
lifestyle of sacrifice and service that we hardly even remember it.
We have it easy. Dishwashing takes place in the dishwasher. The
microwave is taking the place of the oven or the stove. You have a
washing machine and dryer. Only in the poorest areas do you see
clothes hanging on a clothesline. We hardly know what a clothespin
looks like.

We can do it fast now, so it's pot pies, TV dinners, and
McDonald's. Many people don't even know how to cook because

they never had to learn. We can't cook; we can't wash; we can't iron; we can't starch. We're soft! We don't know anything about that tough life back in those days, but in those days we had a better understanding of the basics. Today's women don't have to work hard around the house, and they don't work hard at keeping their marriages together, either. They get offended and leave, when God has called them to endurance and faith.

Faith is a commitment, not just a doctrine. It's a manner of life where you endure all things for the sake of becoming more like Christ—whether you're a woman or a man. God does not ask anything less of a husband than he asks of the wife. He says, *"In the same way, you husbands."*

Husbands commit to their wives
> *"In the same way, you husbands must give honor to your wives. Treat her with understanding as you live together. She may be weaker than you are, but she is your equal partner in God's gift of new life. If you don't treat her as you should, your prayers will not be heard."[29]*

He asks the same of a servant—which all of us are called to be. Think of all the "service industries," where people serve others. From insurance salesmen to waitresses to public officials ("public servants"), our entire civilization functions on the basis of mutual servitude to one another. How much more important should this be in a marriage, where a husband and wife strive to out-serve one another, and in so doing become more like Christ?

PATIENCE IS BETTER THAN DIVORCE

I have been married more than thirty years to the same woman, and most of the leaders and members of my churches are faithful to their spouses in the same way. We do not have the seed of divorce in our ministry. We have the seed of faithfulness to one mate

---

[29] 1 Peter 3:7 NLT.

for life, just like Jesus. We understand the awesome responsibility we have to demonstrate to the world the faithfulness of Christ to the Church. That comes from going after God.

I'm grateful to God that the men and women in our ministry are dedicated to one another for life. These men and women of God have taken to heart the teachings that God has given me and are living the life at home every day. Home is Heaven! It's our place of refuge, refreshing, and refueling. God wants to help you to get the right principles for staying married now so that it won't cost you later. He is preparing you for life in eternity. You get married one time because Jesus is only going to marry you one time. There will be no divorce in eternity. Divorce misrepresents what it means to keep covenant with God. God endorsed marriage from the beginning. He didn't back divorce. If Almighty God doesn't back divorce, neither can we.

Let's say your husband dogged you out. He really criticized you. Maybe you didn't think divorce right away, but you may want to get even with him. I'll let you in on a little secret. if you're patient and let God take care of him, you're going to be much better off in the long run.

Power of patience | *"In your patience possess ye your souls."*[30]

In this world, you'll have the excitement of seeing God move in his life on your behalf. And just in case he doesn't listen, in eternity he might be somebody's slave while you are somebody's king. What you are learning in those places where God has placed you are experiences that will teach you how to think and act like a king. If your husband refuses in his position to be like the king and you take on king-like qualities, then you will be more qualified than he is in eternity. Your patience earns your commendation in Heaven.

---

[30] Luke 21:19 KJV.

> *It's*
> *commendable*
> *to keep on*
> *doing good*
>
> *"But when you do good and suffer, if you take it patiently, this is commendable before God. For to this you were called, because Christ also suffered for us, leaving us an example, that you should follow His steps."[31]*

Adultery and Divorce Mismodel God's Commitment to Us

God marries you for eternity. When a husband and wife stay married instead of getting a divorce when things get tough, they are demonstrating something about the eternal nature of our covenant with God. You are true to your marriage covenant because you represent Christ's marriage to the Church. You don't risk losing eternal rewards and responsibilities by becoming a person who disobeys God.

Since marriage represents the relationship between Christ and the Church, what false impression does divorce give about eternity? That in eternity God might divorce you. There is the potential that you could be married to God and that somehow He might break His covenant. That's not true.

If you are already divorced, God forgives you. Jesus says, "My blood blots out your transgressions, because if I remember that, I can't take you into eternity. The only way I can forgive you is to put it under the blood of forgetfulness." If you are thinking of divorce, think again, and change your thoughts to conform to God's thoughts. He's your husband and He would never divorce you.

> *God relates*
> *to us as a*
> *Husband*
>
> *"For Thy maker is thine husband; the LORD of hosts is his name."[32]*

Some people think that just because they got saved, they're going to miss hell and go to Heaven, and as long as they go to church and be a good person, that's it. Well, you may have eternal life, but that doesn't mean that you're fit to be married to Jesus. Are

---

[31] 1 Peter 2:20-21 NKJV.
[32] Isaiah 54:5 KJV.

you married into His ways? His thoughts? His principles? His lifestyle?

If you don't endorse the principles of the Lord, you won't be a natural match. In the Lord's match, the Husband and the Church will be one. They will be unioned together in one. People who won't give up all their head-tripping and their unwillingness to do the whole Word won't be married to Him. You'll be in the Kingdom. You'll be a child, but you won't be His wife, because He says His wife will not have spot or wrinkle, nor any such thing.

Bride without blemishes	*"That he might present it to himself a glorious church, not having spot, or wrinkle, or any such thing; but that it should be holy and without blemish."*[33]

We have interpreted God's glory as goose bumps, but a glorious Church is not an emotionally driven Church. It is a Bride motivated by character—the character qualities of holiness. The Bible says that the Bride, the new Jerusalem, will make herself ready. That has nothing to do with gender. All of us are Christ's woman. His principles are for the whole Church, becoming more like Him daily in order to be more suited to Him.

When a Christian wife can't get her husband to do what she wants and so she gives up and gets a divorce, she is saying to nonbelievers that God's Word is not good, that God will change His mind. She is acting on the basis of the false presuppositional thinking that when two people get married, they're getting married on the basis of their agreement. And when the two of you disagree, that's how you know you should get divorced. Wrong! That is not a true understanding of the marriage covenant and the heart and mind of God.

In the espousal period, during that time when you're engaged, both of you are faking it. It's not that you don't see things you don't agree with in him; it's just that you let your lust and the potential of staying single prevent you from coming out with the truth before you get married. You're willing to sacrifice for him and

---

[33] Ephesians 5:27 KJV.

not complain about it, but once you know that you have him, then you're offended when he leaves the top off the toothpaste or doesn't flush the toilet or leaves the water running or doesn't put away his shoes at night. If you're not committed to one another to the extent that you're committed to Christ, all of these things become points of disagreement after you're married. You have to overcome them God's way.

The Lord God sets things down in principle. Adultery misrepresents Almighty God in creative order, because Jesus never had sex outside of marriage. We're heading to the marriage supper of the Lamb.[34] He is going to marry the Church. Jesus never once committed spiritual fornication, which is a violation of the covenant standard of God for time and eternity. Jesus never did anything that broke covenant with his Father. He set a standard for His wife. He set a standard for eternity.

How can we have a 50 percent divorce rate in the Church in America? A principle is being violated. Most divorces occur between the third and fifth year. That means your pledge on your wedding day to stay married for life was only good for about three years and you're out of there. While God has given you His eternal word, you won't even make a lifetime commitment.

What you promise should stand the test of time. What you represent should represent eternity, because your foundation is the foundation of the Lord. The Bible says, "For no other foundation can anyone lay than that which is laid, which is Jesus Christ." [35] The only foundation that will stand for time and eternity is the foundation of Christ. It doesn't matter what you or others think. It matters what God thinks and what God established. He established marriage as a lifetime covenant. Your marriage covenant should stand, because the foundation on which it rests will stand.

We Need Mercy and We Need to Give Mercy

Is divorce the unpardonable sin? No. If it's already occurred, Jesus is praying that His blood on the mercy seat will obtain God's forgiveness for you through His death. However, if you need mercy

---

[34] See Revelation 19:9.
[35] 1 Corinthians 3:11 NKJV.

from God, and all of us do, remember to give mercy, especially to your husband.

Be merciful and you will receive mercy	*". . . judgment without mercy will be shown to anyone who has not been merciful. Mercy triumphs over judgment!"[36]*

If you're contemplating divorce, remember this: Whatever you're going through in your marriage, if you are a Christian and you are planning to get a divorce, you are a covenant breaker and God cannot back you. You say, "Why does he treat me so bad? I don't like him. He doesn't like me. He doesn't make me happy." Don't divorce him for that! Give him mercy!

I'm a pastor, so I get amazing complaints from couples. One couple wants to divorce because they don't like the same kind of night out. They want to divorce because they leave hairs in the sink when they wash up in the morning. But the Bible says that "male and female created he them."[37] Your husband is your opposite, so you're not going to agree on everything. That's what puts the excitement in your life! Something happens in a marriage that's dynamic. It perfects you in God and keeps you together. Call on God!

Seek the Lord	*"Seek ye the LORD while he may be found, call ye upon him while he is near: "Let the wicked forsake his way, and the unrighteous man his thoughts: and let him return unto the LORD, and he will have mercy upon him; and to our God, for he will abundantly pardon."[38]*

We are so frail nowadays that as soon as somebody disagrees with us we don't want to be around them. What if everybody had to agree with you and there was a world where everyone looked just

---

[36] James 2:13 NIV.
[37] Genesis 1:27 KJV.
[38] Isaiah 55:6-7 KJV.

like you? Are you so right that God can build eternity on what you think? If not, seek God until the joy of your marriage returns.

Thinking God's thoughts	*"For my thoughts are not your thoughts, neither are your ways my ways, saith the* LORD. *For as the heavens are higher than the earth, so are my ways higher than your ways, and my thoughts than your thoughts."[39]*

The Bible says that Heaven and Earth shall pass away but the Word of God endures forever.[40]

MYSTICAL ONENESS OF A HUSBAND AND WIFE

The oneness that God loves in a married couple represents what He saw when He made man, and what He will see when His Son marries His Bride.

". . . holy Matrimony; which is an honourable estate, instituted of God in the time of man's innocency, signifying unto us the mystical union that is betwixt Christ and his Church."[41]

When God said, "Let us make man," [42] He didn't say let us make man and woman. He said let us make man. He knew in the beginning that He was going to take a woman out of the man. They started out as one, and they become one again through marriage—just like Christ and the Church, His Bride.

---

[39] Isaiah 55:8-9 KJV.
[40] See 1 Peter 1:25.
[41] "The Form of Solemnization of Matrimony" from *The Book of Common Prayer* (1662 Version). Online at http://www.weddings.co.uk/info/wedserv.htm. Accessed July 2012.
[42] Genesis 1:26 KJV.

**They shall be
one flesh**

| *"Therefore shall a man leave his father and his mother, and shall cleave unto his wife: and they shall be one flesh."[43]*

The woman was already there, but she wasn't manifest until God took Adam's side—not just a rib—and she became a woman, a man with a womb. When the woman appeared, she had different properties physically, but she wasn't less than the man in creative order. She had a different responsibility, but the same life. God breathed into the man the breath of life and he became a living soul, so the same life that God breathed into man initially is also that life that enabled woman to be who she is. The life of God came into the woman through the man. She had a different responsibility in God's design, but she had the same life. Male or female, it's God's life that is in your body and in your marriage.

**Oneness of a
man and
his woman**

| *"And God said, Let us make man in our image, after our likeness: and let them have dominion over the fish of the sea, and over the fowl of the air, and over the cattle, and over all the earth, and over every creeping thing that creepeth upon the earth.*

"So God created man in his own image, in the image of God created he him; male and female created he them. And God blessed them, and God said unto them, Be fruitful, and multiply, and replenish the earth, and subdue it: and have dominion over the fish of the sea, and over the fowl of the air, and over every living thing that moveth upon the earth."[44]

---

[43] Genesis 2:24 KJV.
[44] Genesis 1:26-28 KJV.

The Bible says that when the husband and wife get married, they are "heirs together of the grace of life."[45] That oneness goes back to the beginning of creation. When the husband and wife are joined together, they are picturing a union of closeness that existed before God operated on Adam and made the first woman in manifestation. When a man and woman are joined together in marriage, Jesus says, they become as one. He's not trying to get you to figure out how they are one. When God says one, He means one. One in essence. One in understanding. It goes back to creation.

One in Marriage, One In Christ

The husband may have a responsibility different from his wife and a different priority with God related to who usually gets the instructions first, but the husband and wife are one. God created Adam so the man was manifest first, but the woman was in him. She has the same potential. They are one but have different responsibilities and a different physical make-up.

We will be married to Christ. We are one with Him in God. The Church is one with Christ as the woman was one in Adam. That is one in essence. The same life that is in the man is in the woman. She has the same inheritance as the man. We're heirs of God and joint heirs with Christ.[46] I am an heir with Christ because I'm one with Christ in essence. I've been born again not of corruptible seed but incorruptible seed by the Word of God.[47] He's a spirit; I'm a spirit. He has the blood of God in him; I have the blood of God in me. Jesus has the name of His Father. I have the name of His Father. It all came by Christ, because we're going to marry Him. Men and women will have the same inheritance in the next world. That's why the Bible calls us joint heirs.

God decided your gender, so don't get hung up on it. You're not less because of your gender or more because of it. You just have a different application of the same life, of the same oneness, the same essence. God pictures it for us in the natural by saying that when Adam and Mrs. Adam married, the two became one.

---

[45] 1 Peter 3:7 KJV.
[46] See Romans 8:17.
[47] See 1 Peter 1:23.

A husband and wife become one in the natural realm as the Godhead is one in the spiritual realm. In Christ, the husband and wife are qualified to receive the same inheritance.

| **Husband and wife—heirs together of the grace of life** | *"In like manner, ye husbands dwell with them according to knowledge, giving honor unto the wife, as unto the weaker vessel, and as being heirs together of the grace of life."*[48] |

The oneness that a husband and wife demonstrate is oneness in agreement, oneness in mind, oneness in ways, oneness in kindness, oneness in consideration. One, like the oneness in the Godhead—Father, Son, and Holy Spirit.

| **Agreement on one Lord** | *"Hear, O Israel: The LORD our God is one LORD."*[49] |

The new Jerusalem—the bride of Christ—demonstrates Who He is and who we are as the Church. We are one. When you have disunity in your family, you are saying that there is disunity in the Godhead. When you have disunity in the Church, you are saying that the body of Christ is divided. Unity in family and Church speak of Christ.

There is something mystical about our oneness with Christ and a husband's oneness with his wife. It's a real oneness that is as real as what you and I can see now. It's not some kind of idealistic thought. Oneness in God is oneness. If He says in John 17 that you may be one even as I am one with My Father, then that's how together we can be. That takes faith, and it takes commitment.

---

[48] 1 Peter 3:7 KJV.
[49] Deuteronomy 6:4 KJV.

THE PURPOSE AND CALL OF YOUR MARRIAGE

As a wife, you may not fully understand what God is calling you to do, and you may not understand why you have gone through what you have gone through, but when you're a Kingmaker, your husband is on his way to something great because of you. Remember, you didn't take his name because he is all of that. You took his name because you were going to help him be all of that.

A Kingmaker wife can function in a home even when her husband is slightly dysfunctional and has not come up to the level where God has called him. I always emphasize that men are responsible for the spiritual condition of their homes, but in reality women as a group have been the most faithful ones. Pastors take it for granted that the wife will be the more committed believer. She'll bear the burden for the family's spiritual growth. She'll organize family devotions.

When a wife is a Kingmaker who has made Jesus King, she may take on the responsibilities her husband has neglected for a season, but she is not bound by them. She doesn't have to stay in charge. When she sees the least effort by her husband to be the man in the house, she is able to restore him to a place where he once again takes on his family responsibilities. Instead of taking over, she goes low on him. She volitionally puts herself under him, and honors him as her head. She helps him on his way.

Marriage takes maturity

Jesus said, "Not everyone is mature enough to live a married life. It requires a certain aptitude and grace. Marriage isn't for everyone. Some, from birth seemingly, never give marriage a thought. Others never get asked—or accepted. And some decide not to get married for kingdom reasons. But if you're capable of growing into the largeness of marriage, do it."[50]

---

[50] Matthew 19:11-12 *The Message.*

Even when in the natural it seems to a wife that she could do a much better job herself, she allows her husband to function as head in the place where God ordained him to function, because she sees God's big picture for marriage that began in creation. She looks beyond her husband and she sees Christ. She's a mature Kingmaker committed to King Jesus' picture of Heaven in her home.

When your home is like Heaven and your relationship is healthy and growing in intimacy, both of you are becoming strong and sure of yourselves and confident of your relationship as husband and wife for the rest of your lives. Your husband is on his way to achieving his full potential, and your marriage is fulfilling its God-ordained purpose and call.

KINGMAKER CONFESSIONS
Speaking Boldly About Yourself
"David encouraged himself in the LORD his God."[51]

- I endorse the principles of the Lord. I am an ideal match for Him. We are one.
- Our home is a sanctuary. We have Heaven there, and my husband loves to come home.
- I don't think only of myself. I think of God and my husband, making both happy.
- My husband and I have a destiny together in God. I will help him reach that destiny.

---

[51] 1 Samuel 30:6 KJV.

KINGMAKER ACTIONS
Blessed By Doing His Will
". . . a doer of the work will be blessed."[52]

Practice these Kingmaker steps described in this chapter:

1. Greet him with a look that says, "I love you."
2. Fix dinner.
3. Allow him time to unwind if he needs it.
4. Surprise him often as soon as he arrives.
5. Make jokes about your bad days.
6. Keep your home neat and clean.
7. Give your family space to let down and relax.

Describe internal and external steps that you will take to cultivate a greater sense of intimacy in your home.

KINGMAKER PRAYER
Submitting It All To God
". . . not my will, but thine, be done."[53]

In prayer, you become so close to God through experiencing and maintaining His presence that when you get into a situation outside of prayer you are still conscious of pleasing Him, not man. You have to go outside the lines of other people's faith, including your husband's faith, at times. If you stay within their limits, you're trying to please people, but faith is outside those lines. Believe God for great things.

Father, in Jesus' name, I thank You now for the anointing of the Holy Spirit. You've taken my heart and I've given it to You. Oh Lord Jesus, let me know that I am married to You. Let me know that I am one with You. Teach me Your ways. Give me Your thoughts. Bring me up to the next level. The world will say, "Never a woman

---

[52] James 1:25 NKJV.
[53] Luke 22:42 KJV.

spoke like this,"[54] because Jesus is so real in my life. Let me do such wonderful works that only You can receive the glory for it, because it's so awesome. Help me to visualize the new potential in my life. Help me to repent where I need to repent. If I have divorced You, if I have backslidden, restore me now in this moment. May every sick marriage be healed because with Your stripes they are healed. Let every poor person be rich. Let them embrace these principles of God, then live by them. Don't let them feel condemned, but let them be encouraged and restored and then used mightily. In Jesus' name I pray. Amen.

---

[54] See John 7:46.

Chapter 7
The Rebel Husband

"And she was a woman of good understanding and beautiful appearance; but the man was harsh and evil in his doings."[1]

As you recall from Chapter 4, in the days of King Saul of Israel, while David was hiding from Saul, David sent ten men to the estate of a wealthy man named Nabal to ask for food for himself and his followers. Even though David and his men had been doing Nabal a service by protecting his people and his herds, Nabal refused to give them anything to eat. In so doing, he lived up to his name, which means "fool." David was so angry that he was ready to kill him and every other male in the household.[2]

Nabal's wife Abigail was a wise and beautiful woman who realized that her whole family was in danger because of her husband's foolishness. She brought gifts to David and humbled herself and pleaded with him not to harm her husband—not because Nabal didn't deserve punishment but because murder was wrong and it would hurt David's chances for fulfilling his God-given destiny as king.

David said to Abigail, "Praise be to the LORD, the God of Israel, who has sent you today to meet me. May you be blessed for your good judgment and for keeping me from bloodshed this day and from avenging myself with my own hands.'"[3]

As it turned out, David did not have to take revenge. God did. Recall with me what happened next to this rebel husband:

---

[1] 1 Samuel 25:3 NKJV.
[2] See 1 Samuel 25:4-22.
[3] 1 Samuel 25:32 NKJV.

God took revenge instead of David

> *"So it was, in the morning, when the wine had gone from Nabal, and his wife had told him these things, that his heart died within him, and he became like a stone. Then it happened, after about ten days, that the LORD struck Nabal, and he died. So when David heard that Nabal was dead, he said, 'Blessed be the LORD, who has pleaded the cause of my reproach from the hand of Nabal, and has kept His servant from evil! For the LORD has returned the wickedness of Nabal on his own head.' And David sent and proposed to Abigail, to take her as his wife."[4]*

David did not need to kill Nabal, nor did Abigail have to take any action against her husband. God took care of everything because their hearts and actions were right. No husband is so pathetic that a Kingmaker wife can't help him become great. No husband is so great that a Kingmaker can't help him become greater. The resources of Heaven are waiting to back you when you go about it God's way. That's the power you must seek from Heaven.

How Nabal Demonstrated That He Was a Fool
"Nabal is his name, and folly is with him."[5]

- No understanding of the times
- Ignored what he knew
- Didn't take advantage of window of opportunity to serve someone who was helping him
- Didn't sow into the new move of God
- Didn't see with eyes of revelation
- Mismodeled his lineage (he was a descendant of Caleb, one of the heroes who spied out the Promised Land and said it could be conquered)
- Did not set a good example for his children

---

[4] 1 Samuel 25:37-39 NKJV.
[5] 1 Samuel 25:25 KJV.

Should a wife submit to a rebel husband? Yes!

Yes, according to creative order, a wife should submit to a rebel husband. I'm not talking about those few instances where a man asks his wife to kill someone or commit a crime or perverted sex act. Of course your submission to God's moral law would override your husband in every case. There are certainly extreme cases. There are men who beat their wives, harm their children and do other evil acts that must be dealt with appropriately. A man who is physically endangering his wife and children must not have access to them. The New Testament also makes it clear that the innocent spouse is not judged when the other party breaks covenant by adultery or abandonment.

> *However, beyond these extreme cases that may result in long-term or even permanent separation— since none of us married a perfect person— husbands and wives must honor their death covenant by staying married and learning to love it.*

When a husband rebels against God, His Word, and other authority figures in his life, many wives would feel driven to use manipulative tactics in a situation like that. If you are married to someone who is not submitted to God, it is true that you will experience pain. Your hope, however, doesn't lie in numbing that pain with manipulation, fantasy, criticism, or another "coping mechanism." Your hope is in God and the godly methods He gives you to walk out your faith.

Path of Humility

Submission to a rebel husband is a faith walk of humility. You have to be willing to humble yourself and be submitted to your husband as a matter of *principle* even though the brother doesn't have a clue about the right way to act and the right way to treat you. Submission is not something you do by law, but something you do because you have a relationship with God and He gives you an inner witness that it is right.

Your rebel husband is fighting against God. When he acts up and you resist the temptation to raise up against him or manipulate him and instead treat him like the king he's supposed to be, that works him more than if you were running your mouth off against him all day.

The Bible has strong things to say about a nagging wife. God doesn't allow nagging a rebel husband, either!

| *A wise woman builds her house* | *"The wise woman builds her house, But the foolish pulls it down with her hands."[6]* |

You don't want to become one of those nagging wives, regardless of the temptation to straighten him out. The possible benefit of seeing your husband change doesn't justify the means of becoming a witch whenever he's around. When you are submitted to God, your actions, your lifestyle, and your humility give evidence of your subjection, just like Christ who bore our sins on the cross.

OPPORTUNITIES FOR ADJUSTING HIS FAULTS

Humility doesn't mean that you always keep silent about your husband's faults, however. In 1 Peter 3 the Bible says "that he may be won by the conversation of the wives," which you know means lifestyle, but sometimes it means communicating what you receive from God for him. You are talking, talking, talking, and he says, "Honey, would you mind?" Then when he really gets upset with you because you are telling him something again and again, you think, "He doesn't ever listen to me." The brother is listening but he is convicted. He tries to shut you down because he is not listening to the Holy Ghost, and what he doesn't understand is that you are a second Holy Ghost. But woe unto him if you shut up, because if you shut up then the Holy Ghost will show up.

---

[6] Proverbs 14:1 NKJV.

Setting Up the Squeeze Play

When we were first married, my wife and I went through all kinds of struggles. We had our lights cut off, heat cut off, and sometimes could barely buy groceries. Imagine my wife and two children trying to keep warm by the oven while I was out preaching the Gospel and spending my wife's paycheck to pay for the event! I failed her in the beginning of our marriage over and over. I even had to borrow money from her dad. However, my wife never gave up on me, and that has made me the man I am today.

My wife took a risk and walked out her faith in God by submitting to me even though I didn't deserve it. Her attitude helped change me from an undisciplined young husband and father who spent all our money on ministry to the man of God I am today. She humbled herself, and I became exalted. No man in his own right deserves a Kingmaker for a wife. I know I didn't when I married Katheryn. But she believed in me anyway. She saw me for what I could be, and not what I was.

When my wife submitted herself to me when I was out of line, she was lifted up by God.

Lifted up by going down	*"Humble yourselves in the sight of the Lord, and he shall lift you up."*[7]

When a wife goes low on her man, she is under him—exactly the right place to set up what I call a "squeeze play." When she puts herself under submission to her husband, God lifts her up and she carries her husband on her shoulders up to Christ. Meanwhile, the stone (Christ) comes down from above him and falls on the brother. The wife is lifting up her husband, Christ is coming down, and that rebel is caught in a sandwich. That's a squeeze play! It's just what he needs to become changed.

---

[7] James 4:10 KJV.

| *Coming to a place of brokenness* | *"And whosoever shall fall on this stone shall be broken: but on whomsoever it shall fall, it will grind him to powder."[8]* |

The pressure from the wife works only if she is submitted. If she moves outside the realm of the eternal by saying, "I'm not submitting to that rascal," she releases the pressure for the squeeze play that he needs. There is no longer the same leverage for Christ to fall on the man and crush him as she is lifting him up.

God's Commitment to Submitted Women

If you refuse to submit and get in the flesh and start fighting for yourself, you move away from the biblical picture of the Church submitting as the Bride of Christ. You look at your temporary circumstances and judge by what you see, but God is looking at your situation from the view of eternity. He wants your marriage relationship to be a real picture of how the Church submits to Christ.

When a wife is submitted to Christ and to her husband as unto the Lord, God backs her. He protects her from the damage that a rebel husband would do on the inside and outside of her. God is able to do that. He intervened on behalf of Sarah under Abimelech when Abraham told Sarah to submit and go into that harem. The stone of God had to fall on Abimelech and protect her before that king could have sex with her. God knew that Abraham wasn't at the level, but Abimelech got the brunt of it. The Lord not only prevented Abimelech from touching Sarah, but literally came to him and demanded that he release her! Why? Because Abimelech was about to mess with a Kingmaker!

| *Abimelech, you're a dead man* | *"But God came to Abimelech in a dream by night, and said to him, 'Indeed you are a dead man because of the woman whom you have taken, for she is a man's wife.'"[9]* |

---

[8] Ibid.
[9] Genesis 20:3 NKJV.

My wife submitted to me in humility long before I deserved it, and she had strength to persevere. For example, instead of pounding me every Sunday about going to church, she quietly took the children and let me stay home and watch church on TV. At the same time, the power and conviction of the Holy Spirit were falling on me, and once I made up my mind to go to church I've been like a wild man ever since! What my wife did wasn't quick and easy. It didn't prevent her from feeling pain. But it got the job done! She was a Kingmaker.

HOW TO SPEAK AS GOD DOES

There are many ways that God allows you to speak up to a rebellious husband. After all, you may be the only sane voice in the house. However, *how* you say it is sometimes just as important as *what* you say. Make a firm decision during your calmer moments that whatever you say when your husband provokes you to anger will never be something that you later wish you could take back. That knife of rage sticks. Don't use it.

Maybe you have found that when you say something quietly, he just doesn't seem to pay any attention, so you think you have to scream! Maybe he really messed up this time: broke his word, forgot or just plain lied to you, and you want to fight him. Maybe he's been attacking you with criticism, and you feel you must take revenge to survive. Of course, that only makes things worse.

There is a better way. Five is the number for grace. Here are five approaches that can be used by a woman who is full of God's grace when she needs to adjust her rebel husband:

1. Speak with kindness.
2. Speak with the meekness of wisdom.
3. Speak the truth in love.
4. Practice self-control.
5. Use your words to bless people.

1. Speak with kindness. Let's look at the Proverbs 31 woman for a moment in relation to the tone of the words that a wife should use.

| **The law of kindness** | *"She opens her mouth with wisdom,*
And on her tongue is the law of kindness."[10] |

This woman not only spoke with wisdom, but also was governed by the law of kindness. We don't know what kind of husband she had, but it is unlikely that he was perfect, since he wasn't Jesus. Yet she still had a reputation for wisdom and kindness. So will you.

2. Speak with the meekness of wisdom. The Bible says that a person speaking with the wisdom of God speaks with meekness or humility. As you grow personally in the Lord, He will fill you with humility and wisdom and give you the right spirit in situations where you formerly would have been irritable or unkind.

| **Meekness of wisdom** | *"Who is wise and understanding among you? Let him show by good conduct that his works are done in the meekness of wisdom."[11]* |

3. Speak the truth in love. The truth, spoken in love, not only helps the other person who needs it. It also helps you grow up into the Kingmaker role that God envisions for you.

| **Speaking the truth in love** | *"That we henceforth be no more children, tossed to and fro, and carried about with every wind of doctrine, by the sleight of men, and cunning craftiness, whereby they lie in wait to deceive; But speaking the truth in love, may grow up into him in all things, which is the head, even Christ."[12]* |

---

[10] Proverbs 31:26 NKJV.
[11] James 3:13-14 NKJV.
[12] Ephesians 4:14-15 KJV.

4. Practice self-control. Isn't that your goal as a Kingmaker, to grow up and help your husband into headship? Don't let that goal become corrupted by ungodly wrath or unresolved pain! Don't let his negativity take you out of the character of Christ. The woman described in Proverbs 31 was controlled or governed by the law of kindness. She voluntarily submitted to the kindness restriction in her relationships. When you have the fruit of self-control in your life, you don't cross lines. You don't go too far. Ask God to help you to define those boundaries so you know how to react when you face the provocations of a rebel husband.

5. Use your words to bless people. The household of the Proverbs 31 woman was not afraid when she opened her mouth, because she was full of blessings, not criticism. They blessed her in return.

Blessed by her household	*"Her children stand and bless her. Her husband praises her."*[13]

Remember, even if you beat him down and get him to do what you want, his heart is being hardened against you. Do you want him doing right because he fears your wrath, or because he loves you (and God) so much?

MANIPULATION: NOT AN OPTION

In the myths we read as children, the hero slays the dragon and rescues the lady. However, if a woman is not careful in her marriage to a rebel she can be on the side of the dragons—the unsafe methods of manipulation that a wife uses on her husband to get him to do what she wants. Those dragons of manipulation are the opposite of Kingmaking. They are not an option. Unless husbands and wives are mature and consecrated, both are capable of using dragons of manipulation when it suits them. It's usually a quick way

---

[13] Proverbs 31:28 NLT.

to get what you want, relieve frustration, or exact revenge. And just like other quick fixes in life, it's addictive. Many marriages have degraded to the point that neither spouse can make it through a serious conversation without one taking a stab at the other. Like any other addiction, manipulation will kill your most important relationships and ultimately it can destroy any flicker of love and intimacy.

Look at some of the ways that those dragons raise their ugly heads and prepare to slay them!

Manipulation by the silent treatment. When you give your husband the silent treatment, you are saying, "I reject you." The fear of rejection is the biggest obstacle to intimacy in most marriages. The silent treatment takes cruel advantage of our God-given desire for acceptance, and harshly and coldly sends the message "I hate you."

Don't take this lightly. You may get over whatever upset you and feel better and start talking to him again, but the damage is done. You have eroded his trust in you. What does it say about the husband of the Proverbs 31 woman?

| **Her husband safely trusts her** | *"The heart of her husband doth safely trust in her, so that he shall have no need of spoil. She will do him good and not evil all the days of her life."*[14] |

Manipulation by threats. Many wives feel that their husbands don't take them seriously, and unfortunately some of them are right. Others become frustrated with their husbands' failure to follow through on repeated promises. These types of frustration can lead to threats that are designed to scare your husband into an action or to give a quick response. The number one threat is separation or divorce. Some threats are more mild, others more serious.

To be balanced, as I said earlier, there are rare and possibly life-threatening situations when separation or some other unthinkable option must be discussed in a marriage. This can be done honestly and openly without using the option as a manipulative

---

[14] Proverbs 31:11-12 KJV.

tool for coercing a certain response. The presence of a pastor or counselor can help couples sort through these options while minimizing hurt and pain.

Threats are a trick of the devil because they undermine unconditional love and again erode trust. The very idea of threatening to end the marriage or separate suggests "I love you only when you're perfect" or worse, "I'm only committed to you if you do things my way." You may get his attention this way, but you'll never get his heart.

Manipulation by nagging and complaining. Most people think of nagging, complaining and whining as annoying, but not necessarily manipulative. In reality it is manipulative, because its ultimate goal is to make the husband feel like a failure and give in.

Stay positive! Shine!	*Do all things without murmurings and disputings: That ye may be blameless and harmless, the sons of God, without rebuke, in the midst of a crooked and perverse nation, among whom ye shine as lights in the world; Holding forth the word of life.*[15]

More than anything, nagging, complaining and whining sets up a situation where both spouses are miserable. It makes the home a dreary, uninviting place for both of you, not to mention the children. Don't be a drip! Be a flood of living water!

Continual dripping and a contentious woman	*"A continual dripping on a very rainy day And a contentious woman are alike; Whoever restrains her restrains the wind, And grasps oil with his right hand."*[16]

Nagging and complaining may get what you want in the short term, but you will also motivate him to build up ammunition against you! Wearing him down will not make him a king or you either.

---

[15] Philippians 2:14-16 KJV.
[16] Proverbs 27:15-16 NKJV.

Manipulation using sexuality. Manipulation involving female sexuality is both complicated and widely practiced. In this context, many women learn sexual manipulation as a power strategy at a very young age. Even children's cartoons show the villain tricking the hero with an attractive female distraction! The Bible has strong words against sexual manipulation.

| ***Rebellious, seductive woman*** | *"He was strolling down the path by her house at twilight, as the day was fading, as the dark of night set in. The woman approached him, dressed seductively and sly of heart. She was the brash, rebellious type who never stays at home. She is often seen in the streets and markets, soliciting at every corner."*[17] |

Many men act impulsively in response to their sexual desire, and that impulsiveness can be harnessed unscrupulously for gain. Many advertising companies (often run partially or completely by men) use female sex appeal to manipulate men to buy their products or use their services. Of course most of that kind of advertising directly degrades women, but women have often bought into the plan. Not only are there no shortages of actresses and models who will eagerly bare anything for a few dollars, but also women decide to dress immodestly and provocatively on a regular basis, giving the whole town a free show!

Women who use sex appeal to get their own way are unconsciously agreeing with the idea that their other qualities like intelligence, talent, strength of character, etc., are inferior, and so they "play dirty" to win. When these women get saved, they often have trouble defeating the habit of using sex to manipulate their husbands. It's so easy to get even: just kick him out of the bedroom!

---

[17] Proverbs 7:8-12 NLT.

The Bible clearly speaks against this:

Don't deprive him of sexual intimacy	*"The husband should not deprive his wife of sexual intimacy, which is her right as a married woman, nor should the wife deprive her husband. The wife gives authority over her body to her husband, and the husband also gives authority over his body to his wife. So do not deprive each other of sexual relations. The only exception to this rule would be the agreement of both husband and wife to refrain from sexual intimacy for a limited time, so they can give themselves more completely to prayer."[18]*

Manipulation by pretense. A wife who buries her concerns about her husband's shortcomings looks submissive on the outside, but inside she is dying. She is building up painful resentment and bitterness that will ultimately hinder intimacy in the marriage.

Manipulation by outright rebellion. The Bible calls a wife who chooses to lash out at her husband "a brawling woman." When she fights him in the face of his weaknesses she not only hurts him but also undermines his trust in her. If he can't trust her to be merciful when he is vulnerable, how can he learn to listen to what she says?

Brawling woman	*"It is better to dwell in a corner of the housetop, than with a brawling woman in a wide house."[19]*

PRAISEWORTHY WAYS TO DISAGREE

Sometimes women lose on any desire for intimacy when they are continually dealing with their husband's shortcomings.

---

[18] 1 Corinthians 7:3-5 NLT.
[19] Proverbs 21:9 KJV.

They feel that they have only two options: passive compliance or obstinate rebellion. A much better option is respectful disagreement. This is a praiseworthy option approved by God that maintains the relationship while providing a forum for discussion.

| *Praiseworthy woman* | *"Favour is deceitful, and beauty is vain: but a woman that feareth the LORD, she shall be praised."*[20] |

Maybe you don't express yourself well when you disagree with someone, or you don't think well on your feet. Every time you try, it seems to turn out worse, so you keep it inside. You get angry. When you're angry, your spirit isn't quiet. You're mad, and your mind is running away with you. God has an answer to stop this chain reaction. He says you can get rid of rebellion by subjection to honor Christ. You can get meekness worked in you by being submitted to others. You can change your ways and become attractive again.

Respectful disagreement preserves your dignity and sanity, while giving your husband a chance to get it right. To put it simply, you can submit with the right attitude, and respectfully disagree. It is important to express your viewpoint on a matter of disagreement, especially if you turn out to be right. If you respectfully disagree, then he is placed in a much better position to admit his mistake later. If you beat him down with your words, he will most likely remain defensive about the subject, even when proven wrong. That is no way to make him into a king.

Men and women who cannot disagree without verbally assaulting one other are too emotionally immature to be married, or really to be considered adults. Don't allow your emotions or your husband's immature conduct toward you to lower your standards. Find a way to respectfully communicate your point of view while still allowing him to keep his manhood. Remember, you're helping to shape him into a leader and you're acting like a leader who makes others into kings. You're watching out for his blind spots, not

---

[20] Proverbs 31:30 KJV.

attacking him when he's down. You're good to him, and he finds favor with the Lord.

God favors husband of a good wife	*"Whoso findeth a wife findeth a good thing, and obtaineth favour of the LORD."*[21]

God has not set you up to fail, but to triumph. If you have a problem with your temper, go the way of meekness. Put yourself under God's control. When you're in a situation where you're angry enough to lose your temper, choose the way of the Lord, which is meekness—strength under control. When God is in control, you won't use these tactics:

- Win at the other person's expense
- Force someone to admit you're right
- Protect yourself
- Fight back
- Hold a grudge

With God's help you can be a Kingmaker when your husband doesn't come close to being a king. You can have the kind of life-changing faith and spiritual power that will not only help him to find his God-ordained place, but also help him to function properly once he's there. Rest assured that it can be done.

CARRYING HIM BY FAITH IN HIS OFF-SEASON

Every man should have a "God said" for his house. When he doesn't, his wife bears the responsibility by default. Unfortunately, that is what we have in this generation. Many wives have had to pray and get the Word of God for their home. They are the ones who fast more, pray more, and take leadership in instructing the children in spiritual things.

---

[21] Proverbs 18:22 KJV.

Unfortunately, women are more likely than men to be born again, read the Bible, attend church, pray, participate in a small group, and have a quiet time. The result is that in many homes, the woman's faith has to carry the family.

Apparently, this was a problem in New Testament times, too, because 1 Peter 3 is addressed specifically to wives whose husbands were not obeying God: "Likewise, ye wives, be in subjection to your own husbands; that, if any obey not the word, they also may without the word be won by the conversation of the wives; while they behold your chaste conversation coupled with fear."[22]

These verses basically say that if the wife will accept the responsibility to stay in line with God, then her husband can be won. This is serious, because it basically charges the woman to think more about the will of God and the ways of God than even her own self-preservation.

Your Faith-Filled Actions Give Your Husband Hope

The people of faith in the Bible demonstrated a limitless commitment toward God by their faith-filled actions. Peter stepped out of the boat. Moses went to Pharaoh, and before that, his mother disobeyed the law and refused to have the baby Moses killed, because she had faith for her son. The hall of fame of faith-filled people in Hebrews 11 says that they not only had faith but also walked it out with mind-boggling actions.

James said faith without works is dead.[23] You can start by confessing faith, but you demonstrate faith in works when you walk it out in some area that seems impossible to man but is possible with God—like loving a rebel husband.

When you're a Kingmaker with a rebel husband, you have a terrific opportunity to be a woman of faith and power, demonstrating a commitment to God that shows God is real. He's alive! People who see and read God in your life will have hope restored and believe, also.

---

[22] 1 Peter 3:1-2 KJV.
[23] See James 2:26.

What a rebel husband needs more than anything else is a Kingmaker's faith walked out in her submission to him—not because he deserves it but because he needs it and God commands it. When you do something that God commands in spite of what you see, your faith is increased! Your mind is released into the faith realm. You can take a break from analysis. Many actions that do not make sense to the mind are perfectly compatible with the unlimited dimension where God is, and that is where you want to live.

KINGMAKER CONFESSIONS
Speaking Boldly About Yourself
"David encouraged himself in the LORD his God."[24]

- The resources of Heaven back me in tough situations when I go about things in God's way. I need that kind of power right now. God will help me.
- When I am submitted to God, my actions, my lifestyle, and my humility give evidence of my subjection, just like Jesus when He bore my sins on the cross. Therefore, I will submit to God.
- Even when my husband is wrong, the heart of my husband can safely trust in me. For the sake of Jesus, I will do him good and not evil all the days of my life.
- With God's help I can be a Kingmaker even when my husband doesn't come close to being a king. I can have the kind of life-changing faith and spiritual power that will not only help him to find his God-ordained place, but also help him to function properly once he's there.

KINGMAKER ACTIONS
Blessed By Doing His Will
". . . a doer of the work will be blessed."[25]

- Keep a journal to evaluate your daily interactions with your husband.

---

[24] 1 Samuel 30:6 KJV.
[25] James 1:25 NKJV.

- Rate yourself from 1 to 10 or A to C based on the level of
  Kingmaker attitudes you display, especially when you disagree.
- Then describe how you will work to improve your score.

KINGMAKER PRAYER
Submitting It All To God
". . . not my will, but thine, be done."[26]

Why don't we win? Why do we quit so easily? Because we
don't try hard enough to know God and to be like Jesus. We must
consecrate ourselves to everything worthwhile in the Kingdom of
God. If we can focus on a sports event long enough to win, we can
focus on something a lot more valuable—the contest between God
and the powers of darkness that fight us when we try to bring the
kingdom of God in earth as it is in Heaven, beginning with our own
hearts. Do you let inner conflicts stop you in your tracks and make
you start whining that God isn't fair? Or are you in training every
day to be tough, to run your race to win? Jesus said, "Take up your
cross daily." That takes endurance, but you can do it. You can go all
the way to the cross. It's worth it, because that's where the joy is.

Father, in Jesus' name, I thank You and bless You so much. I
thank You that we are the called-out ones, the new generation
church, the last-day church of husbands and wives and single men
and women who do not see themselves by external understanding
but see themselves by creative, spiritual understanding. I will not let
You down. I will fight for my husband, even when he can't fight for
himself. Where I need to get repentance, give it to me, Father. When
I need to admit where I am, help me to take off all the hypocrisy,
Lord, and humble myself. Give me the gift of repentance. Give me
Your blessing. Use me. Send me. Keep me in every way, fighting the
devil away successfully, and staying in Your mercy. Thank You,
Father. I give You praise and honor. In Jesus' name. Amen.

---

[26] Luke 22:42 KJV.

Chapter 8
Kingmaker Mommas

Bill Cosby says that almost every boy who makes his first touchdown in a football game, even after practicing hours with Dad, will look into the stands and shout, "Hi Mom!" We all have a special place in our hearts for Mom. We want her to be happy and approving, and we hate to see her sad or disappointed. Her mood can often determine whether the rest of us will have a good day!

If you're a Kingmaker Mom, your home is a happy one because there's something more important to you than your own pleasure. It's the happiness of your family. As a Kingmaker, you have learned to think outside the box of your daily trials and can focus on the generation your children will live in and lead. Some women literally carry a whole nation, because every president, judge, senator, pastor, and CEO is some momma's boy or girl.

Selflessness gives you options for building relationships. It's a Kingmaker's key to success. If you understand the Cross of Jesus and the call for a Christian to be crucified with Him, you can build a self-less relationship with almost anyone, including your children!

Christ loved me and gave Himself for me	*"I am crucified with Christ: nevertheless I live; yet not I, but Christ liveth in me: and the life which I now live in the flesh I live by the faith of the Son of God, who loved me, and gave himself for me."*[1]

Raising Children Who Love Jesus and You

Kingmakers have the potential to restore a nation to godliness by raising children who love Jesus and their parents. The influence you have over your children today is the influence you have over the leaders of tomorrow. What are you putting into your children's hearts? What kind of example are you providing by your actions?

---

[1] Galatians 2:20 KJV.

Are you teaching them to be selfish or selfless? Are you teaching them to be rebellious or submitted? Do they love God and His Word because you love God and His Word?

In the natural realm, it takes physical sustenance to carry, birth, and nurse a child. If you don't eat and maintain good health while you're pregnant and nursing, your baby will be affected. If you abuse your body with drugs and alcohol, your baby may be horribly damaged or die.

The same is true as you raise your children spiritually. It takes the same level of commitment by a Kingmaker to maintain her spiritual nourishment in order to develop a spiritually healthy child. As a Kingmaker, you have to be able to sustain not only yourself but also those who are dependent on you. Of course this applies to every Christian, but I think you'll agree it has a special and unique application for mothers. Holy mothers are the ones most likely to have holy, obedient children.

| *Holy, obedient children* | *"So you must live as God's obedient children. Don't slip back into your old ways of living to satisfy your own desires. You didn't know any better then. But now you must be holy in everything you do, just as God who chose you is holy. For the Scriptures say, 'You must be holy because I am holy.'"[2]* |

What Do Your Children Hear?

When your children see you face challenges, do they hear you speak faith? Do you lose your cool and say desperately, "I don't know what we're going to do"? Or do they hear you say calmly, "Jesus, you're my Lord. You're my Husband. You're the true and living God. You're my Provider. You're my Protector."

When you speak in faith, you're letting Jesus be Lord of your home from your position of voluntary humility. Christ doesn't just show up in the seasons of prosperity. "Thy Maker is thy Husband"[3] no matter what is going on in your life. Even in the off seasons,

---

[2] 1 Peter 1:14-16 KJV.
[3] See Isaiah 54:5.

Christ is real to you and you make Him real to your children through your humility.

FOCUS ON CHILDREN

Most of the time, mothers as a group are present for far more child-rearing hours than fathers. In the Black American community, a shocking 70 percent or more children grow up with a single-parent mom. Even when there is a father in the home, too often these men don't have a clue. They need a Kingmaker like you in the house.

The presence of a father in the home is so important that all moms should make that a priority of their prayers, but meanwhile they should take their responsibility seriously to build their children into future men and women of God.

During the past 50 years, there has been a great deal of dispute over what motherhood means. As the biblical notion of motherhood has faded from our culture, the duties of moms have been categorized as little more than unwelcome babysitting and maid service.

There is nothing wrong with mothers bringing in income and developing their talents and gifts, as long as you do not depend solely on your work to validate your existence. When you keep your children first even though you work, you bless yourself, your family, and society.

Two generations of women have been taught that they must pursue careers outside the home to validate their identity because being a mom is just not enough to make her feel valued. Other women have been forced to toil to put food on the table because their husbands are unable to earn enough money or are absent altogether. The result of these trends has been to turn the focus of mothers away from home and children. Every woman knows her kids are supposed to be a top priority, but most of the time, the paycheck calls the shots.

Importance of Right Priorities

In other books I have written I have held up a standard of spiritual responsibility for men in the home. Men are biblically responsible to provide financially for the household but they are not supposed to put that job or career in a place of higher priority than their family. Their career should serve the family and their performance at home in turn qualifies them for advancement in the outside world.

Women have the same responsibility to keep their priorities straight. The good news is that there is a new generation of mothers who know how to maintain their priorities while doing everything else that they need to do to support their families. More mothers are working from home, starting home-based businesses and home schooling their children. Many people raising kids today have realized that the "career-first" axioms of the past generation have failed. They are fully committed not only to the idea of parenthood, but also to the process. Many women are managing their homes and raising their kids well. Here are some principles to help.

1. *Maintain your relationship with God.*
2. *Have a daily time of prayer and Scripture reading with your children.*
3. *Put your children on a routine for the day.*
4. *Put the children to bed at a reasonable hour.*
5. *Maintain a balance between planned and spontaneous activities with your kids.*

1. Maintain your relationship with God, even if you have to lose a little sleep to arise early. Spend time daily in the Word of God and prayer. Ask God to reveal His priorities to you and to help you to follow them. Write them down and pray over them daily. If you don't do this, you are setting yourself up to fail. When you pay attention to your relationship with God, other areas of your life will be full of peace instead of chaos and confusion!

2. Have a daily time of prayer and Scripture reading with your children. This can come at the beginning and end of the day and at other times in between. Before your children go out the door to school, they need your blessing and your prayers. Before they sleep, they need the comfort of knowing God is there. When they have disagreements, pray with them and gently admonish them from the Word of God.

3. Put your children on a routine for the day. This is especially important for preschoolers and home schooled children. No successful organization can be run without some kind of schedule, and your family is no exception.

4. Put the children to bed at a reasonable hour. Young children need a lot of sleep and even older kids can be required to go to their rooms and do homework or read at an early hour. If you are single, this will give you private time to regroup. If you are married, this will bring quiet to the house so that you and your husband can have private time.

5. Maintain a balance between planned and spontaneous activities with your kids. Have a plan, but be flexible.

MAKE YOUR HUSBAND A KING TO YOUR KIDS

Being a wife and a mother are complementary roles in a perfect world, but in reality they do require some balancing. Both roles demand self-sacrifice and both offer tremendous rewards. However, both roles can also become tainted by resentment or neglect. Add a demanding job, especially outside the home, and you have challenges.

To be a Kingmaker, you have to stay on top of all of your roles. You can't stumble through your day without a plan and a clear set of priorities and expect things to fall in line on their own. Your husband is the leader, but even if he is doing a great job, he needs you to execute plans consistently if the home is to run the way it should.

Many women today have been taught that a career is rewarding but raising children is drudgery; therefore, they are defeated in their attitude towards the home before they start. Remember this: it can be done! Women through the ages have been faithful wives and mothers in the face of much bigger inconveniences than most of us face today.

Often you're responsible for your children, in a practical sense, for most of the day. Maybe your husband isn't even trying to be involved. Maybe he's gone a lot, but comes home from work and tries to take over and has no idea what he's doing. How can you make him into the king God has called him to be to his kids?

Children need to respect their fathers. Even if he has glaring weaknesses, if you disrespect him or complain about his weaknesses, that will not help your children. It will hurt them. My wife did an amazing job of teaching our children to respect me even when I wasn't paying the bills or taking care of our needs. Their respect and love for me provoked me to grow up and get it together! If your husband does have major character flaws, it is that much more important that you be stable for the sake of your children.

Here are some ways to build up your children's respect for their father and encourage your husband to fulfill his God-given role. You will also find that these habits help your children build the foundation they need for their own happy marriage in the future.

If you are single, be an example to your children of a woman of virtue who is married to Jesus. Don't allow your desire for a man to take you out of the character of Christ in your relationships. Be an example that your children can follow.

If you are married, give your children a picture of a happy, stable marriage. Some women when faced with challenges in their marriage will throw themselves into the kids to avoid the problem. One of your children's greatest sources of security is the strength of your marriage. You owe it to them to do your best to make sure it stays healthy and strong.

Talk to your children (ages four and older) on a regular basis about the importance of your marriage. Use a practical example— Mom and Dad need time together. You don't have to be apologetic, but you should be clear. Remember, your goal is for you and your husband to stay on the same team and to bring the children on board with you.

Spend time talking with your husband about whether your kids' physical, emotional, spiritual and academic needs are being met.

This is your job as parents and God has empowered you to do it. If their needs are met they will not pull on you nearly as much when you need time as a couple.

Ask your husband to help you come up with clear and definable goals for your children. Pray together about these goals. If he doesn't respond initially, bring it up gently at appropriate intervals. If necessary, create a list first and then ask for his input to adjust it.

Ask your husband's advice when you are having a challenge with training the kids. Maybe you don't think he can help, but encourage him to become a problem-solver, and he may surprise you!

Never question your husband's authority in front of your children. Obvious exceptions would include extreme situations where he is clearly endangering them. If you disrespect him in front of the children, repent completely to him and to the kids. Repentance is a sign of spiritual strength, not weakness.

Remind him gently about how much the kids love him and need him. When he's not involved enough, the temptation is to act as if you don't need him. This will not help change the situation for the better. It may seem like more trouble than it's worth, but get him involved in any way you can.

Teach your children how to greet their father warmly and respectfully when he comes home. My wife used to see me coming and call out to the kids, "Daddy's home!" They would run from whatever they were doing and jump all over me. No man can resist that! It makes him more aware of how much he needs to be a dad.

Update your husband on a regular basis (at least weekly) on your children's academic progress. He may not seem interested at first, but see if he will agree to supervise one area of their schoolwork or homework at least once a week. Keep trying different areas until you find a good match.

Encourage your husband to lead a family devotional time at least once a week. You may want to have the kids prepare memory verses or something similar to recite for him during these times. If he is not taking the initiative, watching his children perform may help spark his interest.

Never compete with your children for your husband's attention. They need time with him alone.

Never force your husband to compete with the kids for your attention. The children should be taught to respect your need for time together; however, they should also not feel like intruders in their own home.

Have a set date night on a regular basis. Get a reliable babysitter or ask your parents to fill in, then go somewhere with your husband every week. Dates should be special, but they don't have to be expensive. A date night can even be something you plan at home after the children are in bed.

Encourage your husband to plan family activities and one-on-one activities with the kids. Maybe he can do something as simple as taking them to the store or the auto repair shop. He can attend their sporting events and other performances then take them out afterwards. When children reach adolescence, a special time out with Dad to talk about their sexuality can help them stay pure until marriage. You can never predict how helpful these moments together can be.

Help young children to make a gift or create a card for their dad. Remind and encourage older children to be giving on his birthday or other occasions.

SUSANNA WESLEY: KINGMAKER MOTHER

Susanna Wesley was the mother of nineteen children. Thirteen of them died in infancy or early childhood, which unfortunately was a common occurrence in 18th century Britain. Her six surviving children included John and Charles Wesley. Mrs. Wesley raised her children to love doing what is right. They received a classical education at home and then went to Oxford. There they started a club that became nicknamed the "Holy Club" by the other students because they were so committed to right acts in their personal devotional life and in their organizational focus on serving others. The commitment to righteousness they received from their mother lasted for their lifetime, and has resulted in untold numbers of souls being saved through the Methodist Church that they founded and other denominations that they influenced.

At Oxford, they formed a covenant friendship with George Whitefield, who became the powerful evangelist who helped usher in the First Great Awakening in the American colonies. John Wesley also became an evangelist and preached over 40,000 sermons (many open-air) and traveled over 250,000 miles in his ministry. Wesley never intended to start his own denomination but the mainline churches could not handle his preaching so he organized his followers and the Methodist church began. His legacy remains powerful to this day in countries around the world.

Susanna Wesley was an educated woman, something unusual for women of her day. She knew both Latin and Greek. She was known as a strict disciplinarian but her children had not only respect but also deep affection for her. Her amazing discipleship of her children was captured for history in letters to her sons that reveal a depth of wisdom, humility and strength of character all too rare. She instructed them without compromise with a cutting-edge word that would challenge any pastor or leader today. Her letters touch on virtually every area of life.

Words of Wisdom from Susanna Wesley

Susanna Wesley channeled her personal knowledge of God, education, and strength of character into training and discipling her children, and an entire movement emphasizing the pursuit of holiness was started! No woman should think that raising children is a menial or trivial task! Her children's devotion and passion for the Lord were revolutionary for their time and also made history in the greatest sense of the word. Here is some advice she gave them.

Daily devotions. "Begin and end the day with Him who is the Alpha and the Omega . . . if you do but really experience what it is to love God, you'll redeem all the time you can for His more immediate service. . . . I used to allow myself as much time for recreation as I spent in private devotion."[4]

Humility. "But if after all self-love should incline you to partiality in your own case, seriously consider your own many failings, which the world cannot take notice of because they were so private; and if still upon comparison, you seem better than others are, then ask yourself who is it that makes you to differ, and let God have all the praise, since of ourselves we can do nothing."[5]

Purity. "First, endeavor to get as deep an impression on your mind as is possible of the awful and constant presence of the great and holy God. . . . Secondly, consider often of that exceedingly and eternal weight of glory that is prepared for those who persevere in the paths of virtue. . . . thirdly, meditate often and seriously on the shortness, uncertainty, and vanity of this present state of things."[6]

Motherhood. ". . . there is nothing I now desire to live for, but to do some small service to my children."[7]

Choosing godly friends. "Be very nice in the choice of your company, and never rely upon your own virtue so far as to associate with the vicious and profane. Our blessed Lord, who knew what was in man, commands us to pray daily, 'Lead us not into temptation.'"[8]

_____

[4] Susanna Wesley, *The Complete Writings* (New York: Oxford University Press, 1997), pp. 69-70.
[5] Ibid., p. 73.
[6] Ibid.
[7] Ibid., p. 70.
[8] Ibid., pp. 70-71.

ENCOURAGING CHILDREN TO DO THEIR BEST

When you encourage your children to do their best but love them regardless of their performance that has a positive effect on their advancement. Teach them to strive for excellence and always find something to praise. Children need love and acceptance and somebody to say, "I believe in you," whether they get a good grade or a promotion or not.

Always remain willing to repent to your children when you have missed it with them. That gives them a sense of confidence and safety. As you seek to be like Christ, you will see not only your child's weaknesses but also your own. If you carry a sense of authority from God as a Kingmaker for your children, you won't have to hide your faults to earn your children's respect. God will back you.

KINGMAKER CONFESSIONS
Speaking Boldly About Yourself
"David encouraged himself in the LORD his God."[9]

- I am a Kingmaker to my children. I am able to look beyond my trials and focus on the generation my children will live in and lead. I am carrying the whole nation by what I do, because every president, judge, senator, and CEO is some momma's boy or girl. Why not mine?
- Because I understand the Cross of Jesus and the call to the Christian to be crucified with Him, I can build a successful and selfless relationship with almost anyone, including my children.
- I am maintaining a high level of commitment to my own spiritual nourishment and health so that I will be able to sustain not only myself but also those who are dependent on me. I'm a Kingmaker.

---

[9] 1 Samuel 30:6 KJV.

KINGMAKER ACTIONS
Blessed By Doing His Will
". . . a doer of the work will be blessed."[10]

- Make a list of ways that you can increase the spiritual life of your children.
- Make a list of ways that mothers can teach their children the character qualities of Kingmaking.

KINGMAKER PRAYER
Submitting It All To God
". . . not my will, but thine, be done."[11]

No one likes to hear children whine. We tell them, "Stop whining! I'm not giving you anything when you whine!" When you go to God and say, "Why don't you do this and that," you are whining. You don't give Him an incentive to respond. God can come down and overtake you with blessings. You don't have to whine. Speak to Him in love and blessings will overtake you. Speak in faith on behalf of your children and watch God work.

My Father, in Jesus' name, give me true convictions so that I can consecrate myself and take steps into greater consecration where nothing can influence me to do anything that You have not determined. At this moment, I dedicate myself to You . I only want to do what pleases You. I thank You that You have done marvelous things in my life and the lives of my children. Whatever has been in the way of my children's spiritual development in the past—laziness, powers of darkness, deceiving spirits, lack of knowledge of Your Word, technical knowledge, lack of persevering, lack of training—I declare that all of these problems have been solved, in Jesus' name. I believe you for it. In Jesus' name. Amen.

---

[10] James 1:25 NKJV.
[11] Luke 22:42 KJV.

Chapter 9
Ministry and Marketplace

"Give her of the fruit of her hands; and
let her own works praise her in the gates."[1]

You are more than a Kingmaker to others. Remember that you are also being made into a king. Whether you are single or married, you have a role to play not only in your personal relationships but also in leading your community.

Note that the Proverbs 31 woman's "husband is known in the gates, when he sitteth among the elders of the land" (v. 23). But then the last verse says, "Give her of the fruit of her hands; and let her own works praise her in the gates" (v.31). Not only was her husband known in the community, but also she was known.

While you are growing as a Kingmaker, single or married, you are also being trained and equipped by God to lead as a king. You are called to lead in your local church, your community, your nation, and your entire generation.

In many cultures, women for centuries have been treated like property. They still are in many parts of the world. The feminist movement tried to do away with all gender roles and distinctions to solve that problem and gave us two generations of chaos. But there have always been Proverbs 31 women showing the world what a righteous woman can be and do—a woman who is becoming a king!

DEBORAH: ABLE TO LEAD AS A KING

Deborah is an example of the fact that God is not constrained by gender. He will use anyone to lead whose heart is right and who is willing to go about it His way.

---

[1] Proverbs 31:31 KJV.

Biblical Kingmakers	*"And Barak said to her, 'If you will go with me, then I will go; but if you will not go with me, I will not go!'*
Deborah *Judge Over Israel And Prophetess*	*"So she said, 'I will surely go with you; nevertheless there will be no glory for you in the journey you are taking, for*
Barak would go to war only if she went with him.	*the LORD will sell Sisera into the hand of a woman.'"[2]*

Kingmakers don't seize an apparent opportunity if it means that they have to trash someone else, including a king or their husband and kids, to take that opportunity for leadership. That's like dropping out of medical school to apply for a job as chief of surgery.

The Bible says that your relationships build evidence of your leadership ability. You don't toss out that vital process of self-development that comes from interacting in right relationships with others just because that dream job comes along. Everything has an order and a season. When opportunity knocks it is not always God who is at the door. Sometimes it's the devil.

Will you miss other opportunities if you decide to remain faithful to your Kingmaker roles as a wife or mother or doctor or missionary? Yes, you will. Will that limit God in terms of the greatness you can achieve in His eyes? No!

The quality of your service in your local church, your community and your world depends on your faithfulness to the place where God has called you first.

If some things have to wait, trust God! It's His glory you're working for, remember? You can "have it all" as long as "all" means everything that really matters to God.

---

[2] Judges 4:8-9.

Rising to the true dignity of your nature as a woman— words of Catherine Booth *(1829-1890)* *Co-Founder of* *Salvation Army*	*"The woman who would serve her generation according to the will of God must make moral and intellectual culture the chief business of life. Doing this she will rise to the true dignity of her nature, and find herself possessed of a wondrous capacity for turning the duties, joys and sorrows of domestic life into the highest advantage both to herself and to all those within the sphere of her influence."*[3]

The key to being qualified for kingship is out-serving those you would lead. Jesus said it and lived it.[4] The Son of God washed His disciples' feet yet we think leadership means the right to tell others what to do!

Jesus, our example of servant leadership	*"Ye call me Master and Lord: and ye say well; for so I am. If I then, your Lord and Master, have washed your feet; ye also ought to wash one another's feet. For I have given you an example, that ye should do as I have done to you."*[5]

As a devoted Kingmaker who serves others, you are being perfectly prepared to lead at higher levels. As you serve selflessly with the right heart, you are being qualified in the eyes of God to lead others. Why? Because you take no thought for yourself! You're not doing it for the glory or the recognition. You're doing it to take them where they need to go. That is not only the mark of a Kingmaker making someone else into a king. It is also the essence of what a good king does for his people!

---

[3] Catherine Booth, "Female Ministry—Woman's Right to Preach the Gospel" (her first pamphlet). Online at http://www1.salvationarmy.org/heritage.nsf/0/CCA0EE1FD0DD005680256970004C8225?openDocument. Accessed July 2012.
[4] See Matthew 23:11.
[5] John 13:13-15 KJV.

EMPOWERING THOSE YOU LEAD, AS JESUS DID

One of my assignments from God is to raise up leaders. Sometimes people who want something from me will tell me, "I'm called to be with you," but they say it for a lot of different reasons. Some said it to me decades ago, before I had any recognition, and they have stayed with me through the trials. Others see me on stage before thousands or on television and think that means I'm successful or anointed. They think they can use me as a stepping stone to their own fame.

In a purely practical sense, those men and women who are called to be close to me get the advantages of what God has done in me and through me. They get access to meetings they wouldn't be allowed into otherwise and hear information they wouldn't otherwise hear.

Why do I take them into those meetings and places? I am called to carry them someplace that they couldn't get to on their own. I'm a Kingmaker. I allow people to tap into my resource base—spiritually, strategically, and financially.

Think about the Christian TV personalities. How many have a number one disciple who goes with them everywhere to learn everything they know and become greater than they are? The truth is that most of them aren't going to take that disciple along with them and give them that level of exposure. In many cases when they take somebody with them on ministry outings they use them strictly to serve them and carry their bags. They have no intention of sharing their resource base and training others to replace themselves. They may even spiritualize it this way: "I worked real hard to get to where I am and if you work real hard God will get you there, too."

That is not how Jesus did things! He didn't draw people around Him just so that they could help Him fulfill His personal goals! He didn't command us to "make personal assistants." He commanded us to make disciples! In fact, He promised, "The truth is, anyone who believes in me will do the same works I have done, and even greater works, because I am going to be with the Father."[6]

---

[6] John 14:12 NLT.

Jesus had no ego issues with those under Him getting greater fame and recognition and doing even greater miracles than He did!

The average pastor would not be excited if somebody under him said, "I'm going to do greater works than you." However, I am being honest with you when I say that it brings me great pride and joy when I see one of my disciples preaching before crowds or on television or hearing people testify about how much that person has meant to them. I am overjoyed that many of the young men and women in my ministry have awesome marriages right from the start, without the trials my wife and I had to endure. Now, I've had disciples leave me, too. Sometimes it's just time to move on, other times it has been with a wrong attitude. Even when those people have left me the wrong way, I have blessed them. Many times I have seeded into their work financially but always I have blessed whatever they were doing as long as it was in line with the Bible. That is what Kingmakers do. Kingmakers carry people to places they can't get to on their own. They love and bless them unconditionally.

PERSONAL EMPOWERMENT

If you haven't done so already, start taking steps to realize your call to leadership as much as you understand it. *(See "Receiving Empowerment From God" below.)* This may or may not mean that you are becoming a minister or climbing the corporate ladder in the traditional sense. However, you are trying to make yourself available to the Lord to use your talents and gifts in any way He desires so that you can be a Kingmaker to others. Ask Him for the discernment to know what that means on a practical level. No one ever made forward progress by just thinking about it. You have to take action steps. Ask God what those steps are.

You will be a Christ-like leader in the ministry and marketplace if you take aggressive steps for your own success as you are inspired and empowered by God. These steps relate to your long-term growth, and will prevent you from becoming a Christian who starts strong yet falters at the end. You are a finisher!

Study your areas of interest. Read books on topics that are important to you. Consider furthering your education in Bible school or college or take advantage of opportunities available in local technical schools or community colleges or distance education on the Internet. Sign up for training opportunities that your local church, denomination, or ministry association may offer. Sometimes the answer to your prayers is just that close!

Stay informed on the issues. Stay up to date with the news, especially on issues that concern you. Be sure that you are registered to vote and participate in all general elections. Pray about becoming involved in the political process beyond just voting.

Guard against deception. Clearly, deception is something wise women guard against. Both men and women can be deceived but God does give specific warnings to women. The Bible reminds us that while Adam sinned willfully, his wife was deceived.

Woman deceived	*"And Adam was not deceived, but the woman being deceived was in the transgression."[7]*

The Bible speaks of false teachers who fool silly women:

Foolish women	*"For of this sort are they which creep into houses, and lead captive silly women laden with sins, led away with divers lusts, Ever learning, and never able to come to the knowledge of the truth."[8]*

Following the principles I have outlined above will help you to protect yourself from the deception of the devil and put you on the alert against the common lies he throws at women of God.

---

[7] 1 Timothy 2:14 KJV.
[8] 2 Timothy 3:6 KJV.

Deceptions from the Devil

"Put on all of God's armor so that you will be able to stand firm against all strategies and tricks of the Devil."[9]

- I don't have time to read the Word and pray.
- _____ *(person's name)* is holding me back from being great and achieving my best.
- If I just had ____ *(more money, more time, more influence, etc.)* I'd be happy with my life.
- If I could only _____ *(lose weight, have better clothes, etc.)* I'd be happy with myself.
- My problems are worse than anyone else's because _____ *(fill in the blank)*.
- It's understandable for me to get in the flesh with my husband/children because _____ *(fill in the blank)*.

Obviously, there are many other excuses. Develop a list of your own in your devotional time and then make a commitment to stop listening to the devil and to go the way of the Lord.

RECEIVING EMPOWERMENT FROM GOD

When you build up your spiritual foundation first, you can lead in the world from that same foundation. To a spiritual woman, there is no separation between church and state or marketplace and ministry. She functions as if God owns it all, because He does. And as if Christ is Lord of all, because He is. Submit your visions to God without conditions and receive His unlimited empowerment.

Pray for vision and obedience. Pray about your passion and role in your family, church, community and generation. Pray in the Spirit and with your understanding.

---

[9] Ephesians 6:11-12 NLT.

	"Wherefore God also hath highly exalted him, and given him a name which is above every name: That at the name of Jesus
Bowing before	*every knee should bow, of things in*
that name	*heaven, and things in earth, and things under the earth; And that every tongue should confess that Jesus Christ is Lord, to the glory of God the Father."*[10]

Cultivate the presence of God in private devotions. A strong leader needs strong faith. You need to know Jesus Christ intimately as your Husband and Friend. God's Word is your reading matter of choice. His company your highest joy. If you have not already done so, get a copy of my book *My Journey with God* as a guide to the self-discipline you need to develop your personal consecration. These days you must be both consecrated and disciplined in the marketplace and ministry. *My Journey with God* includes a 30-day journal where you can document your prayers, your Scripture reading and your revelations, and become personally accountable before God for your daily life.

Learn to forgive and release hurt. If you're the kind of person who remembers every bad thing said or done as if it were yesterday, you will not get far in serving the Lord. Pain is part of life and relationships. Most people you love will hurt you at some point but that doesn't have to be the end of the world. You can either accept it and deal with it or spend all your time licking wounds.

	Jesus said, "And whenever you stand praying, if you have anything against anyone, forgive him,
Forgive and you	*that your Father in heaven may also forgive you*
can be forgiven	*your trespasses. But if you do not forgive, neither will your Father in heaven forgive your trespasses."*[11]

---

[10] Philippians 2:9-11 KJV.
[11] Mark 11:25-26 NKJV.

RECEIVING EMPOWERMENT FROM FAMILY

If you are single, share your vision with your parents and mature Christians like your pastor and elders. You're never too old to honor your father and mother. That is one of the Ten Commandments that never goes out of style. God gave your parents to you and He can continue to use them in your life as long as they are on the earth.

Honor your parents	*"Honour thy father and thy mother: that thy days may be long upon the land which the LORD thy God giveth thee."*[12]

If you are married, develop an understanding with your husband about your role outside the home. In the early years of my married life, I sent my wife to work while I called myself "doing the ministry." She was supporting the family without her total agreement. That cost me. Why? I took advantage of my freedom as the man. She was submitted to me and I took advantage of her to do what I wanted. Now, am I saying that women should quit your jobs and not work? No, I'm saying to keep the right perspective.

When a husband and wife are dedicated to God, the woman is not working just so that the two of you can have a higher standard of living. Men who don't have a revelation or a vision from God to be supported by their wives should get a job and have the testimony of being financially responsible in the house. They misrepresent God if they don't work and God is not in it.

Sometimes we men can get super-spiritual and say, "I just have to do what the Lord is leading me to do. I know what you're saying, Pastor, but I have to obey His will for my life." Meanwhile, everybody is talking about your family, talking about you, you old lazy thing, you, and you are talking about how "the Lord is leading me to do something else instead of work." You are putting that woman through pressures you are supposed to be handling as a man.

In some instances, because of his educational level or the current job market, the man you married is not able to make much

---

[12] Exodus 20:12 KJV.

money to support you. So in that instance, because the two of you are going in a certain direction, you say, "Well, Honey, I can see working to help support the family." If the man is responsible under God he will say, "If you're seeing it, that will help us to progress." Then together you set a vision and a goal for you to progress as a family. In that situation, you are working with your husband not just to make money but to get into a position to fulfill destiny and represent the highest standard of a Kingmaker. You share the responsibilities of home and children because you share a destiny.

If you have children, put them before work. No God-ordained opportunity will cause you to neglect your ministry to your family. That doesn't mean that you couldn't work out arrangements for your children that free you to work in the marketplace or ministry, but simply that you make *them* your priority, not your job. You stay alert to signals of problems at home. Your family is first according to God's creative order. Not only that, but God gave them to you as a blessing. If you have too much stress or too much unrest, go back to God again and see if your timing might be off. You might start a home-based business or minister from home so that your children can stay in the forefront of your life.

A young mother might say, "Where would I ever find the time to pursue a ministry or go into the marketplace?" Obviously, caring for children involves a lot of time spent teaching and nurturing them as well as chauffeuring them all over town. However, remember that they will leave the nest someday and so while they take up a great deal of your life now, they cannot "be" your life. Take the time to pursue these other interests as long as they are in harmony, not competition, with your home ministry to your children!

RECEIVING EMPOWERMENT FROM CHURCH

Women are uniquely qualified for leadership in the church. When you are a committed believer, serving the needs of the Body of Christ is a natural next step. The best place to begin is in your church.

Catherine Booth, co-founder of the Salvation Army, said this:

| *". . . we cannot discover anything unnatural or immodest in a Christian woman . . . in a pulpit."*

 Catherine Booth
 (1829-1890)
 Co-Founder of
 Salvation Army | *"Making allowance for the novelty of the thing, we cannot discover anything either unnatural or immodest in a Christian woman, becomingly attired, appearing on a platform or in a pulpit. By nature she seems fitted to grace either. God has given to woman a graceful form and attitude, winning manners, persuasive speech, and, above all, a finely-toned emotional nature, all of which appear to us eminent natural qualifications for public speaking."*[13] |

Learn leadership by submitting and serving actively in your local church. Serve as a committed member of a local church where you honor the leadership. If you are submitted to a local church or denomination that does not permit women to preach that must be your standard. Find an area where you are needed or have an interest. This is a great first step for developing your leadership potential for future responsibilities outside the church, as well.

Develop your potential by coming under the covering of your local church. Walking around trying to lead people without having the spiritual covering of a church is a dangerous thing. I meet men and women all the time who have strong talents, gifts and callings that will never be fully realized because they can't submit to God as He is working in their lives through their pastor and local church leadership. Don't allow impatience or pride regarding your church leaders to disqualify you from fulfilling your potential!

---

[13] Catherine Booth, "Female Ministry, or Woman's Right to Preach the Gospel." Online at http://www.indiana.edu/~letrs/vwwp/booth/ministry.html. Accessed July 2012.

RECEIVING EMPOWERMENT FROM OTHER WOMEN

The New Testament records some disputes between women in the early Church but it also gives a clear message about the advantages of female friendships in the Church.

Respect aged women. The Bible says that aged women have a duty to be just as consecrated and full of wisdom as men are in the church and they are also to be treated with just as much respect as you give your mother. Chronological age doesn't necessarily indicate wisdom, nor does youth mean ignorance, but be secure enough to allow older women you trust to help you evaluate yourself and grow.

Respect women in the church as mothers and sisters	*"Treat older women as you would your mother, and treat younger women with all purity as you would your own sisters."[14]*

That word "older women" in that verse is the same word used for ruling "elders" in verse 17. They are worthy of great honor.

Double honor for elders who rule	*"Let the <u>elders</u> that rule well be counted worthy of double honour, especially they who labour in the word and doctrine."[15]*

Build open and vulnerable relationships with mature women who can provide you with counsel, mentorship and encouragement. Younger women who form friendships with older Christian women receive invaluable input for their development that they should receive graciously. The same applies to other areas where one woman needs the wisdom of an aged mother in the Church. They have the wisdom and the honor of their age.

Maintain fellowship with spiritually like-minded women. Reach out to unsaved women, but do NOT surround yourself only with carnal

---

[14] 1 Timothy 5:2 NLT.
[15] 1 Timothy 5:17 KJV.

friends. They will sap your anointing! When you are with your friends, are you more likely to pray or gossip? Do your friendships center around spiritual growth or the latest entertainment? Do you make fleshly compromises? Would Jesus do what you do?

Don't allow yourself to become competitive with other women.
There is more than enough room in the Kingdom of God for everyone to become great. A true friend rejoices in another's blessings as much as her own. Someone else's joy or success adds to yours! Ungodly competition and envy are rooted in insecurity and the habit of comparing yourself to others. Don't be a separatist.

Become a mature woman whom others respect. Scripture clearly tells seasoned women to teach the younger. Mature women have a God-ordained destiny to bishop and teach younger women. Men and women need their wisdom. They are serious about God. They have a good time but they know that this is not religion. This is reality. When young and foolish women are having sex outside of marriage, it's time for a real mother to step in. She may not be the girl's biological mother, but she is willing to take her on and bring her under subjection.

Older women reverent, teachers of good things	*". . . the older women likewise, that they be reverent in behavior, not slanderers, not given to much wine, teachers of good things—that they admonish the young women to love their husbands, to love their children, to be discreet, chaste, homemakers, good, obedient to their own husbands, that the word of God may not be blasphemed."[16]*

Make yourself available to minister to younger women, but don't derive your identity or sense of worth from their respect for you.
Women who "need" to be needed or admired set themselves up for disappointment. If you focus on living a genuine Christian life, disciples will come! Be a Kingmaker.

---

[16] Titus 2:2-5 NKJV.

FIND YOUR PASSION AND GO AFTER IT

It is always the right time to ask yourself questions that provoke you to spiritual passion. Who are my spiritual children? Whom can I influence? Whom am I called to lead? Isn't my character worth multiplying on the earth? Does your commitment to Christ qualify you to lead other men and women because of your dedication to God? What can God show them in your life that will help them? Are you virtuous? Do you have a sense of holiness?

As you seek God, take responsibility for your personal growth and relationships, and strive for excellence in every area of your life, something will surface as a special talent or gift that you should develop. When it does, then go after it and be blessed.

KINGMAKER CONFESSIONS
Speaking Boldly About Yourself
"David encouraged himself in the LORD his God."[17]

- I am more than a Kingmaker. I am being made into a king.
- I am being trained and equipped by God to lead as a king.
- I am called to lead in my church, my community, my nation, and my entire generation.
- I am a Kingmaker who serves others, so I am being perfectly prepared to lead. As I serve selflessly with the right heart, I am being qualified in the eyes of God to lead others.
- Because I am building a strong faith, I am becoming a strong leader. I am always seeking to know Jesus more intimately as my Husband and Friend. God's Word is my favorite reading material. His company is my highest joy.

---

[17] 1 Samuel 30:6 KJV.

KINGMAKER ACTIONS
Blessed By Doing His Will
". . . a doer of the work will be blessed."[18]

Write down how you will take the following steps to becoming a Christ-like leader in ministry and marketplace:

- Pray. Cultivate the presence of God in private devotions.
- Learn to forgive and release hurt.
- If married, develop an understanding with your husband.
- If single, share your vision with your parents and mature Christians like your pastor and elders.
- If you have children, put them first.
- Develop leadership skills first in your local church.
- Stay informed on the issues.
- Study your areas of interest.
- Take steps to fulfill your destiny.

KINGMAKER PRAYER
Submitting It All To God
". . . not my will, but thine, be done."[19]

God has all the power you need to overcome the world, the flesh, and the devil. The power of God is available for you to overcome the world, but first you have to overcome the world in you. You are made of flesh, but your spirit can overrule your flesh.

The devil has been restrained. Nowhere in the Bible does it say to respect the devil. You *disrespect* the devil. You respect God and godly people. Refuse darkness from this hour forward. Receive a divine release from every bondage, every hindrance, and every bit of guilt that is within you. Be healed of your sins. Be a real Christian. Stand up for Christ as never before.

You won't get promoted by God if you rely on your own effort. Joseph did not do one thing to get out of his slavery other than being a man of God. His attitude and his fellowship with God in the

---

[18] James 1:25 NKJV.
[19] Luke 22:42 KJV.

midst of his circumstances proved that he was promotable, and God did it for him. Take risks in prayer. The generation needs you.

Father, in Jesus' name, I am asking You to perfect that which is lacking in me. If I could do it in my own strength, I would be perfect. You prophesied that You would return for a glorious church. I want to be in that number. Go on and finish Your work inside of me and help me to do what is pleasing to You. I want to please You. I want You to be able to move me in any direction. You said that Your people would be willing in the day of Your power. Put a divine willingness in my heart to know what is a God-said for me and be willing to die for it. I want to go for it in a perfect sense and not shrink away. I want to be like You in every thought, word, and deed. In Jesus' name I pray. Amen.

Chapter 10
Treating Your
Guests Like Kings

"Be not forgetful to entertain strangers:
for thereby some have
entertained angels unawares."[1]

If you watch kids, you'll notice that some love being home and are always inviting their friends over. Others never want to stay home. What makes them congregate at another family's dinner table? True, some may want to go to the house with the pool table or the best video games, but for kids it's ultimately all about love. The quality of the Christ-likeness in family relationships makes them love their home.

Do you like the environment that you're creating in your home? If not, how does that affect your husband? Your children? Your guests? In this chapter you will find many practical ways that a Kingmaker like you can create a home full of hospitality with an environment that energizes everyone who comes.

In Titus 1:8 and 1 Timothy 3:2 the apostle Paul lists "being given to hospitality" as a qualification for leadership in the church. Now this makes sense if we understand what a later verse says, "For if a man know not how to rule his own house, how shall he take care of the church of God?"[2]

The dictionary defines hospitality as the "cordial and generous reception of guests." So the Bible is telling us that the quality of our leadership ability is shown by how well we are able to receive guests who live outside our home!

---

[1] Hebrews 13:2 KJV.
[2] 1 Timothy 3:5 KJV.

Given to hospitality, serving the saints

> *"Be kindly affectionate to one another with brotherly love, in honor giving preference to one another; not lagging in diligence, fervent in spirit, serving the Lord; rejoicing in hope, patient in tribulation, continuing steadfastly in prayer; distributing to the needs of the saints, given to hospitality."[3]*

HOSPITABLE SINGLE: HENRIETTA MEARS

You don't have to be married to be flowing in the gift of hospitality. One of the most influential single Christian women of the past century was Henrietta Mears, director of Christian Education at Hollywood Presbyterian Church, where she was a spiritual mom to future leaders like the late Bill Bright and his wife who founded Campus Crusade for Christ. She also had a profound influence on Billy Graham and was a great encouragement to him. Campus Crusade for Christ has reached billions with the Gospel of Jesus Christ and billions more have been touched by Billy Graham. That is Kingmaking on a mega scale!

Henrietta and her sister Margaret purchased a large home in Hollywood for the express purpose of reaching the rich and famous with the Gospel as well as saving and discipling the youth of Hollywood Presbyterian Church.

Miss Mears bought beautiful furnishings and continually stocked the house with lavish provisions for the multitude of dinners, parties, and meetings that were held there. An energetic woman with a great sense of humor and a wild taste in hats, she was always the perfect hostess as she maintained the tradition of Christian hospitality of her mother, grandmother, and great-grandmother before her.

Miss Mears said, "Hospitality should have no other nature than love." Here is the way she explained her motivation:

---

[3] Romans 12:9-13 NKJV.

Christians dedicating their homes to Christian fellowship increase their influence, said Henrietta Mears (1890-1963)

Former Director of Christian Education, Hollywood Presbyterian Church, Hollywood, California

"If Christians would only realize the powerful influence that entertaining in their homes could have on those around them, there would be far more gracious home entertainment by Christians than there is. When a person has been in your home and eaten at your table, he feels a close bond with you; he feels as though he really knows you. Christ did much of His work in the homes of the people. If more Christians would dedicate their homes, their dining tables, their living rooms to inviting others to partake of Christian fellowship with them, the effect would be tremendous. . . . As soon as the members of a church begin to use their homes for Christian entertaining and as centers for Bible study groups and prayer groups, then the church will have the vitality of an early Christian church and the influence will increase tremendously."[4]

HOSPITABLE WIFE: EDITH SCHAEFFER

Edith Schaeffer is the widow of one of the greatest Christian thinkers of the 20th Century, Francis Schaeffer. They met in a church theology debate and later married and moved to Switzerland. In 1955 this American couple opened their chalet to intellectuals searching for truth. They called it L'Abri, which means "shelter."

Over the next few years, the Schaeffers reached people who had rejected Christ with their minds but ultimately gave in because God touched their hearts *and* minds through the Schaeffers in their home. They offered hospitality but demonstrated that hospitality and love do not require compromise on biblical principles.

---

[4] Barbara Hudson Powers, *The Henrietta Mears Story* (Grand Rapids, Michigan: Fleming H. Revell, 1957), p. 53.

Teaching children that people are important	*"What is a family? A family is a formation center for human relationships. The family is the place where the deep understanding that people are significant, important, worthwhile, with a purpose in life, should be learned at an early age. The family is the place where children should learn that human beings have been made in the image of God and are therefore very special in the universe."*[5]
Edith Schaeffer Co-founder of L'Abri in Switzerland, widow of theologian Francis Schaeffer	

Thousands of people came and went from Francis and Edith Schaeffer's chalet, ate her home-cooked food, enjoyed her hospitality, and were instructed in the Word of God by her husband. She set a precedent for her generation and those who followed for home-education of children and home-based care of the sick and elderly. She also authored several books while running the house and entertaining her guests.

In her book *The Hidden Art of Homemaking,* she encouraged women to look for excellence and beauty in every area of daily home life: cooking, baking, letter-writing, music, gardening, and more. Her life and writings demonstrate the life of a Kingmaker who knows how to bring Heaven to her home.

Edith's ministry of hospitality was the perfect complement to her husband's ministry of apologetics. Her love and faithfulness to her husband's vision augmented his great mind. The resulting synergy produced a lot more than a few meals and a well-kept house. Her efforts provided an environment where her husband's leadership could shape the direction of the Body of Christ in their generation.

HOSPITALITY TO BUILD THE CHURCH

Good old-fashioned hospitality is not a relic of past generations. It's actually a biblical mandate! We've lost the front porch mentality of my mother's generation when everybody could visit everybody else's house any time. Now we hide in the back

---

[5] Edith Schaeffer, *What Is A Family?* (Grand Rapids, Michigan: Baker Book House, 2000).

patio and complain if anybody drops in to see us at dinner time. It's time to reverse that trend and put out that welcome mat again.

Hospitality without grumbling	*"And above all things have fervent love for one another, for 'love will cover a multitude of sins.' Be hospitable to one another without grumbling."*[6]

The hospitality of individual households overflows in explosive church growth. When you have Heaven in your home and share it with others, the good fruit of your ministry spills over into your church and your community.

Invite close family and friends, but also branch out to other people who need your light.

Heart full of light	*". . . now you are full of light from the Lord, and your behavior should show it! For this light within you produces only what is good and right and true."*[7]

The Greek word for fellowship is *koinonia*. Loving *koinonia* and sharing one's home are at the heart of the Christian message.

Fellowship in one accord, breaking bread from house to house	*"And they continued steadfastly in the apostles' doctrine and fellowship, in the breaking of bread, and in prayers. . . . So continuing daily with one accord in the temple, and breaking bread from house to house, they ate their food with gladness and simplicity of heart, praising God and having favor with all the people. And the Lord added to the church daily those who were being saved."*[8]

---

[6] 1 Peter 4:7-10 NKJV.
[7] Ephesians 5:8-9 NLT.
[8] Acts 2:42, 46-47 NKJV. The Greek word for "fellowship" here (underlined) is *koinonia*.

When you practice *koinonia* like the early Church, you don't have to entertain every night and you don't entertain beyond your budget. You are sharing what you have, not showing off. You are creating an environment that draws people to Christ through you.

STEPS TO IMPROVING YOUR HOSPITALITY

Married women who are making their husbands into a king are making him into a leader. Helping him lead *at home* is the first step because he proves himself by leading you and the children. That includes hospitality. Leading *from home* is the next step!

The Schaeffers' ministry, which continues to touch nations after his death, began when they opened their home to intellectuals and others who needed to talk about their faith in God, or their lack of it. They found in Francis Schaeffer a man of God who had something they needed and in his wife a woman who honored and respected her husband and also welcomed them into their home.

Respecting your husband in front of your guests	*"Nevertheless let each one of you in particular so love his own wife as himself, and let the wife see that she respects her husband."[9]*

Helping your husband to become a king in his home, as Edith Schaeffer did, means that you empower him to lead *at home* and *away from home*. Next to raising your children, practicing biblical hospitality is a great team ministry to be birthed from your marriage!

Making a new beginning for hospitality

Below are eight ways that you can make a new beginning in the area of hospitality and, if you are married, empower your husband to lead in this area. The list is followed by additional insights for you on each point.

---

[9] Ephesians 5:33 NKJV.

1. If you are married, submit your plans first to your husband. If you live with your parents, consult them.
2. Prepare a few special guest meals at home.
3. Learn about place settings and other formalities
4. Keep it simple.
5. Do it often.
6. Don't keep score.
7. Show guests that you respect your husband.
8. Present an example of a godly marriage.

1. If you are married, submit your plans first to your husband. If you live with your parents, consult them. You can show respect for your husband's biblical place if you don't schedule guests in the home without his knowledge or against his will. Unless you're Abigail and he's Nabal, there's no reward in Heaven for that. This consideration also applies to your parents, if you live with them.

2. Prepare a few special guest meals at home. The meals don't have to be gourmet but they should be appealing. Of course, if you really hate cooking and can afford it, buy some nice carry-out food and maybe make the dessert!

Simon's mother-in-law healed, then showed hospitality to Jesus	*"Jesus . . . found Simon's mother-in-law very sick with a high fever. 'Please heal her,' everyone begged. Standing at her bedside, he spoke to the fever, rebuking it, and immediately her temperature returned to normal. She got up at once and prepared a meal for them."[10]*

3. Learn about place settings and other formalities from books and magazines if you haven't been taught. You don't have to be formal but it never hurts to know etiquette. Add your own special touches that you can teach to your children.

4. Keep it simple. You don't have to throw huge parties unless that's something you and your husband both enjoy and do well.

---

[10] Luke 4:38-39 NLT.

5. Entertain often. In general, it's better for relationship-building to have smaller gatherings on a regular basis than to host one large get-together once a year.

6. Don't keep score. You may find that as you practice hospitality the way the Bible commands that you have more guests than returned invitations.

Giving and receiving abundantly	*"If you give, you will receive. Your gift will return to you in full measure, pressed down, shaken together to make room for more, and running over. Whatever measure you use in giving—large or small—it will be used to measure what is given back to you."*[11]

Remember that it's a ministry and something you're doing unto the Lord. You're not doing it to get paid back. Ultimately, when you have Heaven in your home, your family will be refreshed and renewed from spending time there and so will your guests. Your husband will learn to lead effectively in your marriage as a father and as a host. With practice, your family can minister to your church, your community, and ultimately your generation!

7. Show your guests that you respect your husband or parents. Involve your husband in helping serve the your guests and ask him to give the blessing over the meal. Seat him at the head of the table. Make him look like a king before his guests!

Demonstrating holiness in public subjection to your husband	*"For after this manner in the old time the holy women also, who trusted in God, adorned themselves, being in subjection unto their own husbands."*[12]

Honor your parents in the same way. Be an example of God's best.

---

[11] Luke 6:38 NLT.
[12] 1 Peter 3:5 KJV

| *Living long by honoring father and mother* | *"Honour thy father and thy mother: that thy days may be long upon the land which the LORD thy God giveth thee."[13]* |

8. Present an example of a godly family. Let your guests go home convinced that they have seen a genuine example of people in harmony with one another through Christ. Don't feel obligated to expose your home and family to dangerous or disreputable people unless that is your calling and safeguards are in place. Maybe you are not called into full-time ministry in the traditional sense but you are called to touch and change lives through your hospitality.

KINGMAKER CONFESSIONS
Speaking Boldly About Yourself
"David encouraged himself in the LORD his God."[14]

- I am conscious of the need for hospitality in my home. Therefore, I will create an environment like Heaven.
- I realize the powerful influence that my home can have on others, so in my home others are always welcome.
- I have so much love for others that my love can cover a multitude of their sins.
- I will be hospitable without grumbling. I will remember that when I'm entertaining others I'm also entertaining Jesus.

KINGMAKER ACTIONS
Blessed By Doing His Will
". . . a doer of the work will be blessed."[15]

- How would you teach younger and less experienced women the social graces—how to prepare for guests and how to treat them in the home? This may include the areas of food (shopping, cooking, serving, cleaning up); preparing the environment (cleaning,

---

[13] Exodus 20:12 KJV.
[14] 1 Samuel 30:6 KJV.
[15] James 1:25 NKJV.

adding pleasing odors such as scented candles and flowers);
setting out fresh bed linens and towels for overnight guests;
adding special touches (fruit bowls, nuts, candy).
- Would people from around the world want to come to your house,
  as they came to the chalet to see the Schaeffers?
- Do you create a home environment that draws people or do *you*
  need to get out of the house all the time yourself?
- How can you take steps to change?

KINGMAKER PRAYER
Submitting It All To God
". . . not my will, but thine, be done."[16]

We are ordained to clear the atmosphere over neighborhoods,
cities, and nations through prayer. We cast down strongholds and
bring thoughts into captivity.[17] If we have power over every thought
that means lives can be changed by what happens in our homes.

Father, in Jesus' name, show me whom I should serve in my home
today so that I can be more like You. Help me to serve somebody
today who won't appreciate what I do and never look for their praise
but only for Yours. Make me willing to be used. Help me to be a
bridge. Give me the grace to let people walk all over me if it helps
them get to You. I confess that sometimes I've been acting like a
snake and striking back. Give me the strength to be a worm who is
willing to be crushed. Thank You for using something I did to show
others in a dramatic way that You are a real and loving God. In
Jesus' name I pray. Amen.

---

[16] Luke 22:42 KJV.
[17] 2 Corinthians 10:5.

Chapter 11
Becoming A
Person of Influence

"Likewise, ye wives, be in subjection to your own husbands;
that, if any obey not the word, they also may without a word be
won by the conversation [lifestyle] *of the wives. While they* [the
husbands that are obeying not the word] *behold your chaste*
conversation coupled with fear."[1]

Picture this scenario. A husband and wife, Judy and Tom, are discussing their need to do a better job having a family devotional time. Not surprisingly, Judy brings it up first. "Tom," she says, "we need to do devotions more consistently with the kids."

"Sure, Baby, I think that's a good idea," he answers.

She says, "Well, I think we should commit to doing it Monday, Wednesday and Friday, and I'll just order this book that I found online today."

"Sure, that sounds fine," he agrees, and that is that.

On the outside, there is nothing wrong with this conversation. There is no fighting or even disagreement. Judy probably felt that if she didn't "take charge" her husband would never decide when to have family devotions and what book to use, let alone implement the plan. And in some ways she might be right.

In the short term, Judy gets what she wants and what she believes that the Lord wants yet in the long term she has set up her husband to become more and more passive regarding the spiritual growth of their family. Instead of asking his opinion and assessment of the situation and by doing so serving as his Kingmaker and encouraging his leadership she has asked him to "rubber stamp" her

---

[1] 1 Peter 3:1-3 KJV.

plan. She needs to learn about the Kingmaker communication skills that I am about to give you in this final chapter.

I believe that almost everyone would like a good marriage or an ideal friendship or job where everybody gets along. They just don't know how to do it. I have found during more than 30 years of ministry that most men want to be good husbands and most women want to be good wives. Most employees want to serve their employer. However, most marriage relationships and workplace scenarios haven't progressed beyond each person bargaining and negotiating to get their own needs met.

In a tense marriage, the husband looks out for himself, the wife looks out for herself, and the intimacy, trust and joy that God intends for both of them are lost. Marriage is supposed to be a win-win proposition based on the Word of God, not a competition for a bigger slice of the pie! In the Church, you don't win points with God for disputing with the pastor or talking behind his back. Life is not a war. You don't have to kill the competition. You're trying to make things better—for everyone.

WIN-WIN COMMUNICATION

What you are about to read will show you how you can be a win-win Kingmaker communicator who increases her influence and productivity as a wife, mother, career woman, sister, or daughter, and helps someone else become all that he or she can be as a King.

It's All In The Presentation
There will be times when you need to bring up not only new suggestions but also areas of weakness or fault to your husband, your friend, or your boss. As marketing experts would say, "It's all in the presentation." If you can do a good job presenting your information, the other person just might listen. Don't allow a bad presentation to ruin the opportunity to share some advice that the Lord has given you for someone else!

If my wife wants to serve me a piece of cake, she brings it on a plate with a fork and napkin on the side. She doesn't pick it up and smear it all over my face, like you sometimes see couples do at wedding receptions. That too often serves as a bad omen for arguments to come.

Kingmaker communication is built on the biblical picture of Jesus Who came to do the will of His Father. He died for us and ever lives to make intercession for us. Unless you have died to yourself and live for God, your desires will not always be God's desires. A Kingmaker is willing to submit her desires to God first to find out if what she wants is want God wants. When she gets into a discussion (or flat-out argument), she doesn't have to win to build her ego. She wants the other person to win, too, because she has his best interests at heart. She is a Kingmaker helping him to become a king.

| ***Trusting God and submitting to His ways*** | *"Trust in the LORD with all your heart, And lean not on your own understanding; In all your ways acknowledge Him, And He shall direct your paths."[2]* |

Women hold positions of power and influence in the world today more than ever before. Women have proven to meet just about every challenge put to them in the workplace, and increased influence has resulted. This is certainly not a bad thing in itself, but feminism tells women that *self-promoting* professional influence is more desirable or more valuable than the *selfless* influence God has ordained for them to have in the home, church, or marketplace. Fame and power cannot replace the warmth and comfort of a family and true friendships the way God has ordained it. A corporate position is a cold substitute for a God-ordained, love-filled relationship.

Interactions in marriage, family, and friendships shape your attitudes. If you manipulate, fight and yell at home, you are likely to do the same thing in the workplace or church when given any latitude or power. However, if you learn how to interact and influence God's way in your marriage and family relationships, you will be well-equipped to handle almost anything that comes your way outside!

God has given women the power of influence from the beginning. That influence is a responsibility from God to be

---

[2] Proverbs 3:5-6 NKJV.

stewarded. God releases a measure of power to you, but He won't necessarily prevent you from misusing it, because He has given you a free will. Mrs. Adam had influence over Adam, and she used it wrongly. Now Adam was still responsible for his decision, but that doesn't change the fact that his wife's influence had far-reaching implications for all of humanity. God held her accountable, also. There were consequences that women are still dealing with today. Reread Genesis Chapters 1 to 3 and you will see what I mean.

SOMEBODY'S WATCHING YOUR LIFE

Here's a Scripture that shows clearly that God wants wives to reach their husbands with lifestyle instead of words:

Winning respect without a word

> *"Likewise, ye wives, be in subjection to your own husbands; that, if any obey not the word, they also may without a word be won by the conversation* [lifestyle] *of the wives. While they* [the husbands that are obeying not the word] *behold your chaste conversation coupled with fear."[3]*

The Bible doesn't say *"if* they behold your chaste conversation" but *"while."*

I want you to know that when you think your husband (or someone else you want to make into a king) is not paying any attention to you, he is actually watching you intently. This verse is talking about unsaved husbands! Someone may resist your "religion," but he can't ignore the way it affects your life.

The Bible is literally exhorting women married to unsaved men to be in subjection to them and also live the Christian life before

---

[3] 1 Peter 3:1-3 KJV.

them with a submissive spirit. You see, feminism has taught you that if you submit to your husband that he'll never respect you; you have to "make him" respect you. But that is not what this verse is saying. Respecting your husband actually challenges him to respect you!

Adorned with a meek and quiet spirit

"Whose adorning let it not be that outward adorning of plaiting the hair, and of wearing of gold, or of putting on of apparel. But let it be the hidden man of the heart, in that which is not corruptible, even the ornament of a meek and quiet spirit, which is in the sight of God of great price. For after this manner in the old time the holy women also, who trusted in God, adorned themselves, being in subjection unto their own husbands."[4]

God wants to use your marriage to test and increase your integrity. He wants to give you influence, but He will not look the other way with your hypocrisy. So many women think they are right because they compare themselves to their husbands or to the average Christian. Yet God evaluates you by your conscience and His standard, and He will only release godly influence to you as you progressively yield to His way! He wants people to be won through your blameless lifestyle that proves Jesus is Lord!

Only Jesus Can Satisfy You
When you are unhappy about the way someone treats you, don't let your emotions cause you to take your focus off God and His assignment to make him into a king. Your goal is someone else's change—in spite of the way that person treats you. Many women complain that their husbands don't make them happy, as though God gave you a husband so that you could be fulfilled. Church members complain that the pastor doesn't treat them right, and leave. Your fulfillment comes in satisfying your Creator.

Many "Christian" wives enter matrimony more in love with the idea of being married to a man who can meet their needs than

---

[4] 1 Peter 3:4-6 KJV.

with marrying someone as a result of being in love with Jesus and fulfilling destiny. Sorry! That is a set up for continual dissatisfaction!

If you expect your husband, pastor, or boss to give you all of the positive reinforcement that you crave, think again. The only person who can satisfy you is the One who created you. You'd better figure out how to focus on God to fulfill you, and stay faithful to Him in what He has called you to do! That will give you a lot more grace to put up with someone's shortcomings as you try to make him into a king.

You Don't Have to Fake It to Make It

As a Christian, you get upset when you fake it and misrepresent God, because you know that is not the real you. By the grace of God, I went from a "humble upbringing" (or the ghetto, as I call it!) to speaking live before more than a million people for the Lord. I don't speak the king's English that well, and it might have been tempting for me to try to fake it in those circles. But why would I do that? God has taken me this far by His sovereign hand! Why would I try to do something on my own now?

That's what the Bible is talking about when it says not to try to influence your husband by external beauty like your hair or your makeup or your clothes. How can a woman who faked it during courtship and won her husband by her beauty get angry when he's superficial in their marriage! She can't understand why he starts looking around when she gets sloppy and loses that fashion model's edge. Come on, girl. You were asking for it. But you can change!

If you try to advance in the corporate environment by sexually stimulating your boss, you can forget about getting God's backing. You force Him to come against you. In the Kingdom of God, you're beautiful because of your integrity and inner attributes. Those qualities give you real influence. Those qualities can win a person's heart!

Maintaining Your Influential Edge

God is calling women to a new level of power that can change others' opinions of them without their opening their mouths. The Bible says to be subject. That's what it says. Follow the instructions. It's like buying a new computer. If you don't follow the instructions on the CD you can't load the software onto the computer. It won't work.

When God talks about being subject He's not talking primarily to your mind. He's talking to your Spirit. He's dealing with your will. King Jesus in the Kingdom of God is telling you to be subject. This is not optional if you want the results that God says He is going to give you if you do. He says, "Be subject. I'm commanding you, be subject!" If you can't see yourself going under subjugation—like a slave, no less!—and you immediately try to figure out another plan, you'll lose your influential edge. You'll have to resort to fleshly power and manipulation to get your own way.

If you have the attitude that you will agree with what God says regardless of what your mind says, He'll work out the practical aspects in terms of how it applies. But until He can get your attitude and your will in line, He cannot release power to you. If you stay obedient to what He has commanded you to do—be submitted—you will prove to Him that you can handle real power.

You Don't Have To Use Your Mouth

If you use your *behavior* to influence someone, you won't have to use your *mouth*. The biggest problem of most women, including Christ's Woman, the Church, is their mouth. The Bible says that you shouldn't use your mouth for both blessing and cursing,[5] and you won't do that when you have the Spirit of Christ.

Woman, God is calling you to a new level of power where *you don't have to say a word.* You can change your husband or your boss with your behavior because the power of God is at work in your obedience. When the Bible talks about subjugation of a wife, it compares that to a slave's subjection to a master. It is the difference between a low look and an evil eye.[6] It goes beyond being humble to

---

[5] See James 3:10.
[6] See Mark 7:22.

being humiliated. Subjugation deals with humiliation. We're talking extremes here, but in order to get extreme results you have to use extreme means.

GRANDMA HAD HER HUSBAND'S RESPECT

Our grandmothers never had to worry about getting more influence over their husbands. They respected and served their husbands, and therefore they had favor with them. I remember how the old mothers used to put liquid starch on their husbands' shirts, then hang them up to dry with clothespins on a clothesline outdoors. After they dried out, those shirts would be stiff as a board. The women didn't have a can of spray starch. They had to sprinkle those hard shirts with water, roll them up to keep the moisture in, then iron them. They didn't resent it. They just did it, and they did it in advance, before their husbands needed them. They planned ahead. They would wash, sprinkle, starch, and iron shirts for their husbands, themselves, and their families for the whole week—out of respect for what their husbands had to do.

Today a man goes in the closet and looks for a shirt and there's nothing there. He says, "Where's my shirt? Where's my underclothes and T-shirts? Where are my socks?"

His wife says, "Look in the clothes basket." And he goes to look in the clean clothes basket but she says, "Oh, I mean the dirty clothes basket." Actually, the washing machine hasn't been turned on for a week. She hasn't taken the responsibility of going to the cleaners. She says, "You mean I've got to wash clothes this week?"

Grandma Didn't Complain
I'm talking about a mentality. In your grandmother's day, women wanted to serve their husbands. They worked much harder than we work today, both physically and mentally. Today we complain a lot about communication. "My husband won't talk to me." "My husband isn't interested in me." But in those days a man would go out to work and his wife would serve him and nobody complained about their tough life. They just lived the life the best way they knew how, and thanked God for it.

I remember working outdoors with my grandfather. He would cut down wood and sell it. We had a wood stove that sat in the middle of the living room, and many times we even cooked on it down there in Clinton, North Carolina. Many people had wood stoves to heat their houses and cook, so he could earn his income by cutting wood. He would go out and work all day long cutting wood and then come home exhausted. He was not going to sit around the fireplace and watch TV, even if he had one. He was so tired he could hardly stand up. He couldn't sit down. He had to flop down.

Do you think my grandmother would come to him and complain? "You don't care anything about what I did all day. I had a rough day, too, you know." These days if the man had money he would say, "O.K. You had a rough day. Go see a psychologist. There's the checkbook."

No wonder Jesus ever lives to make intercession for us. God wants you so dedicated to others as a Kingmaker that you say, "God, if You want to use me, use me. I am not carrying that emotional baggage any more. I am getting rid of those attitudes. I'm yours. Tell me what to do." If He assigns you to a husband or boss who takes advantage of your time, you don't care. You're just being obedient to your Lord. You're not existing for what you get out of this life. You're focused on the rewards of the next life. You want to be prepared to marry Jesus, so you do on-the-job training *now*. God calls you, and you become His responsibility. You trust Him. You believe in Him. If He says it in His Word, that's it. You say, "I'm going to do what He says the best way I know how. He'll protect me with his angels and keep me from making a mistake. If I do and I discover that it's wrong, I'm going to repent and go right on."

What did Grandma used to say? "Daughter, you don't have no common sense." Where are the Kingmakers who are that bold today? Who can tell you when you are whining and complaining about whether somebody treats you right that what you're saying just doesn't make sense? Who can tell you to quit complaining about your condition and get up and do something for God by serving somebody and doing what he needs? Grandma, where are you?

ABC'S OF CONFLICT RESOLUTION

God has given us clues about how to influence other people without whining or manipulation. You can be the real thing and get things done! The number eight signifies a new beginning. Under the heading "Prepare To Be A Person Of Influence," I give you eight points for a new beginning for yourself before you face a confrontation with someone. Under "Maintain The Right Approach," I give you eight points for a new way of approaching someone within a conversation. Finally, there is a three-point close.

ABC's of Conflict Resolution

"But if you are willing to listen, I say, love your enemies. Do good to those who hate you. Pray for the happiness of those who curse you. Pray for those who hurt you."[7] *—Jesus*

A. ANTICIPATE that you will influence someone.
B. BEGIN with the right approach.
C. CONCLUDE with a win-win for everyone.

Your influence will be increased as you line up with what God has said and submit to those in authority, without trying to resist, dominate, or manipulate.

A. ANTICIPATE THAT YOU WILL INFLUENCE SOMEONE

These eight steps will help you to become a woman of influence:

1. Put in quality time praying and reading God's Word.
2. Set a goal of building a better relationship.
3. Keep your sense of humor. Don't take yourself too seriously.
4. Put yourself in the other person's shoes.
5. Make a list—not only what you want to change in someone else but also what you see that's right.

---

[7] Luke 6:27-29 NLT.

6. Keep the devil and your fleshly emotions out of this discussion.
7. Build confidence that you will have God's wisdom.
8. Focus on eternity.

1. Put in quality time praying and reading God's Word. Prayer gives God an opportunity to talk to you (if you listen) and to move on your behalf before you say a word. If you don't take the time to seek the Lord and find out what He is really saying in your situation, you are enslaved to what you see going on in the natural realm. Michal spoke with the same authority as if she had been praying and fasting and seeking God, but she was speaking not to make a king but to bring a king down!

2. Set a goal of building a better relationship. Set your goal higher than trying to resolve differences on one issue. Use differences of opinion to build your relationship and also become a better person yourself through the interaction.

3. Keep your sense of humor. Don't take yourself too seriously.

Stay cheerful!	*"A merry heart doeth good like a medicine: but a broken spirit drieth the bones."*[8]

God is in a position to hear people disagreeing with Him at the highest level—the heads of nations, and He laughs!

Get like God. Laugh!	*"He who sits in the heavens shall laugh."*[9]

4. Put yourself in the other person's shoes. How would you like to have someone speak to you when you're down and feeling especially vulnerable? Would you like to hear words that stab you like a knife, or something embracing that shows they see where you are? Think

---

[8] Proverbs 17:22 KJV.
[9] Psalm 2:4 NKJV.

about what the other person is going through all of the time that you are speaking to him.

> ### How To Put Yourself In Someone Else's Shoes
> *"Look . . . every man also on the things of others."[10]*
>
> - Listen to him. Get to know what he thinks about, what interests him, his goals, his preferred friends.
> - Learn about how she spends her time, her hobbies, her favorite books, music, TV shows, and web sites.
> - How long has he been a Christian? What biblical teachings has he been exposed to? What is the religious influence of his parents and friends? Where does he go to church? What are his goals for his personal devotional life? Has he read the Bible?
> - Learn about her financial management, attitude toward debt, spending and saving habits.
> - Learn how he likes to explore new information: heated discussions with others, classes, reading, radio, Internet, newspapers, magazines.
> - Stay alert for hidden agendas, assumptions, unmet needs.

As Christians, we should be the most merciful people on earth because of the mercy shown to us by Jesus. We should bear their infirmities as our own, just like Jesus.[11]

Esteem others higher than yourself	*"Any story sounds true until someone sets the record straight."[12]* *"Let nothing be done through strife or vainglory; but in lowliness of mind let each esteem other better than themselves. Look not every man on his own things, but every man also on the things of others."[13]*

---

[10] Philippians 2:4 KJV.
[11] Isaiah 53:12.
[12] Proverbs 18:17 NLT.
[13] Philippians 2:3-4 KJV.

5. Make a list—not only what you want to change in someone else but also what you see that's right. Identify what points are convictions that *must* be changed and which are personal preferences with several options. You are not going to compromise if the other person asks you to sin or wants you to allow him to sin without interference. However, other areas might relate to a different way of doing something. Maybe you like to hang the toilet paper roll so the paper comes over the top and he likes to hang it so that the paper comes out the bottom. Some disagreements have no more substance than that. That's ridiculous!

6. Keep the devil and your fleshly emotions out of this discussion. My son once asked me the question, "Why didn't God kill the devil?" I answered, "Son, that was so that you could have devil practice." The only good purpose that the devil has in the earth is that our interactions with him show us how much we are like God and how much we resist Him.

You authenticate your reality as a spiritual being made in the image and likeness of God when you defeat the devil and resist your flesh. The devil may attack you in your emotions, but you prove out your Christianity when you resist him and he flees! Many times the spiritual battle for your spiritual life is won or lost on the battlefield of emotions. The devil has the advantage of accusing the brethren day and night before God. He fights to keep your perspective skewed toward this present moment because he knows that if you saw what he saw in the future, you would always obey the Lord!

There are times that submitting to someone in order to be their Kingmaker boils down to controlling your emotions in the midst of a tense situation. You don't get "in the flesh" when you should be "in the spirit." Gaining control over your emotions is vital to increasing your influence in your home and beyond. This doesn't include only emotions that cause you to lash out, but also those that cause you to withdraw, such as depression or anxiety. The Bible includes emotional control as a standard for leaders:

Slow to anger,	*"He that is slow to anger is better than*
ruling your	*the mighty; and he that ruleth his spirit*
own spirit	*than he that taketh a city."*[14]

When you have control over your emotions, you may still *feel* them but you are not ruled by them. They don't dictate your words, your responses or your decisions. They are not acting independently from your spirit and mind. How does greater emotional control cause your influence to increase? For one thing, people can trust you more readily when they know that you won't fly off the handle or sulk for days. For another, it allows God to give greater weight to your words when He knows they won't be based solely on emotions. What would have happened if Samuel got in a bad mood one day because of his frustration with Saul's attitudes toward God and decided to attack him with a tirade of emotionally charged words? Could God have backed him in the same way?

7. Build confidence that you will have God's wisdom. Of course the other person wants to hear what you have to say, because you have God's wisdom and their respect. When you know that you have the right to speak based on your relationship, you expect that what you have to say to them will count for something. You don't go after that person with a hostile attitude or let negative emotions hurt your credibility and obscure the points you want to make.

8. Focus on eternity. Don't focus in the realm of externals, of earth-based, superficial things! You are making this person into a king for eternity! Maybe he doesn't make a lot of money, but he feels more like a man of God than someone who is a multi-billionaire because you treat him like a billionaire! You treat your boss as if she were important to you, because she is! You see her beyond where she is and you treat her as she is going to be! You remember that God is watching and He will determine your status in eternity based on what He sees now.

---

[14] Proverbs 16:32 KJV.

B. BEGIN WITH THE RIGHT APPROACH

1. Begin your conversation humbly and positively, not aggressively.
2. Phrase your points as concerns, not criticisms.
3. Keep to your point.
4. Be slow to speak.
5. Be quick to listen.
6. Stay positive and don't push.
7. Emphasize your common interests and goals.
8. Be willing to admit your weaknesses to the other person.

1. Begin your conversation humbly and positively, not aggressively. Encourage the other person to come up with ideas that will help resolve the situation. You know what will happen if you explode like this: "You never talk to me and I am dealing with such and such a mess and you're not helping me at all!" Forget that. The other person will put up her defenses right away. Instead, be gracious. Say, "Do you have a minute? I need your help to find a solution to a problem I'm having." That opening will make your words much easier to deal with, and you might learn something.

Talking it out to build a relationship	*"As iron sharpens iron, a friend sharpens a friend."*[15]

2. Phrase your points as concerns, not criticisms. Saying "I'm concerned we may be spending too much" sounds a lot better than "You're wasting money!" Most people are at least part way reasonable. They usually don't have to be jumped on to get the point. Work with them!

3. Keep to your point. Don't allow a flood of side issues to cloud the discussion on the main point and for the most part deal with one problem at a time! Don't allow yourself to be distracted by a flood of emotion. Focus!

---

[15] Proverbs 27:17 NLT.

4. Be slow to speak. Remember when David was coming home to bless his household and Michal cut him off with criticism? Some wives cut their husbands short by running their mouths before the husband's blessing can be spoken over them and then they don't repent afterwards for their hasty words. Few men have the internal resolve to be able to bless someone who is always attacking them. That's logical, isn't it? There are too many Scriptures to cite about watching what you say. All of us understand that words have power and that once they are spoken and heard they cannot be unsaid. Many men and women run their mouths in an effort to influence others but did you know that the Bible says that limiting and controlling your words will actually increase your influence? That is what this chapter is about.

The Lord did not let any of Samuel's words fall to the ground. God literally backed every single thing he said! How can you get that kind of anointing, that kind of credibility? It starts with being slow to speak—curbing that instinct to open your mouth and staying quiet no matter how badly you want to say something. Train yourself to be quiet and pass up some opportunities for you to talk, then see what happens.

None of Samuel's words fell to the ground	*"So Samuel grew, and the LORD was with him and let none of his words fall to the ground. And all Israel from Dan to Beersheba knew that Samuel had been established as a prophet of the LORD."[16]*

5. Be quick to listen and slow to get angry. Listen politely to the other person. If you ask a question or make a point, be still and allow him to speak. If he interrupts you, don't drown him out. Give him the floor. The more you listen, the more you will get to know him and understand why he makes the decisions he does.

Slow to get angry	*"My dear brothers and sisters, be quick to listen, slow to speak, and slow to get angry."[17]*

[16] 1 Samuel 3:19-20 NKJV.
[17] James 1:19 NLT.

6. Stay positive, speak softly, and don't push. Show the other person the esteem you have for him or her. Take time at the beginning of your conversation and as you talk to praise and affirm the other person's good qualities. Keep your tone positive and whatever you do, don't whine! Keep building him up while you're presenting your points—not to manipulate him but to keep your perspective right. Don't push her into a corner, or she will have to fight you to get out. Have you ever seen those big trucks with the sign on the back that says "Do Not Push"? That may be a word for you to heed.

| **Soft answer** | *"A soft answer turns away wrath, But a harsh word stirs up anger."*[18] |

Remember that if you beat the other person to a pulp you may win for the moment, but you both lose in the end. If you make your point and she's able to receive it, you both win!

> ***Before you speak to someone, stop and think.***
> ***Are your words shaping them into a king?***
> ***Are you speaking like a Kingmaker? Are you***
> ***encouraging them to do things that will strengthen***
> ***their spiritual walk, or are you criticizing them?***
> ***Will what you are telling them make them more***
> ***righteous? Will it make them more of a***
> ***man or woman of God?***

7. Emphasize your common interests and goals. You must have some points of agreement with this person or you wouldn't be in this relationship in the first place. Don't focus on your differences. Focus on your agreement, then look for areas of common ground even in the areas you want to see changed. Don't fight as if you're in competition and determined to win. Work with her as a friend whom you want to keep as a friend forever.

---

[18] Proverbs 15:1 KJV.

8. Be willing to admit your weaknesses to the other person. Think about your weak areas and how they affect your words. Are you telling your husband to get you a larger house? Are you telling him to get you a new car, more furniture or new decorations for the house? If you are always spending money, maybe you get a rush from shopping that you aren't getting in prayer. You have money in a bag with holes in it, and you'll never be satisfied. Be slow to make demands if you haven't checked your heart with God first!

C. CONCLUDE WITH A WIN-WIN FOR EVERYONE

1. Know when to quit. Before you get too emotional or the other person gets too agitated, it's time to be quiet and quit.
2. Make sure that everyone wins. Graciously give the other person credit for some good points.
3. In unresolved situations, ask for outside help.
4. Never become a dripping faucet. When it's over, it's over.

1. Know when to quit. Before you feel yourself getting overly emotional in your conversation, quit. If the other person is becoming agitated, quit. Politely end the conversation before you both say something you'll regret.

| **Leave off contention** | *"The beginning of strife is like letting out water, so quit before the quarrel breaks out."[19]* |

2. Make sure that everyone can win. In summarizing your conversation, graciously give the other person credit for some good points. Mention that both of you have gained points. There should be a win-win conclusion to this discussion. Hopefully you have been open enough to learn something, and so has she. Thank her for giving you new insight on this matter, and mean it. Remember that if you beat the other person to a pulp, you may win for the moment, but you both lose in the end. If you make your point and she's able to receive it, you both win! Your goal is not the destruction of the

---

[19] Proverbs 17:14 NLT.

other person. You want her to remember this conversation—not for the level of strife but for the level of helpfulness.

3. In unresolved situations, ask for outside help. If you follow these principles consistently and the other person still becomes defensive or won't listen, you may need a third person involved, preferably a pastor or Christian counselor.

If he will not hear, you may have to consult someone else	*"If he hears you, you have gained your brother. But if he will not hear, take with you one or two more, that 'by the mouth of two or three witnesses every word may be established.'"*[20]

4. Never become a dripping faucet. When it's over, accept the fact that it's over. If you still hold a grudge and keep harping until the other person gives in, God won't bless that kind of persistence.

Constant dripping	*". . . a quarrelsome wife is as annoying as constant dripping.'"*[21]

It is sometimes better to let someone get away with something for the moment than to stay on them and risk displeasing God.

BUILD A BRIDGE AND GET OVER IT

When my wife and I got married, her mother gave her some very good advice. She said, "Katheryn, if you two get in an argument, I don't want to hear about it, because you'll forgive him and forget about it, but I'll still be mad!" My mother-in-law was referring to the old-fashioned assumption that in any marriage there will be disagreements and problems but both parties are expected to get over it!

In reality, nobody's perfect. We all cause offenses. Jesus said, "Offenses will come."[22] In the real world you deal with

---

[20] Matthew 18:15-17 NKJV.

[21] Proverbs 9:13 NLT.

[22] See Matthew 18:7.

offenses but you have to find a way to get along. As my wife says, "Just build a bridge and get over it!" The hardest part of building a bridge is starting it. You have to get something over that water or between those cliffs before you can build the road. That takes planning and ingenuity. It might look impossible, but engineers do it all the time.

Stay positive and assume that you can build a bridge in any relationship. Assume that the other person will work with you. While you're building out a bridge from your side of the river, he will be building one out from his side and you'll meet.

KINGMAKER CONFESSIONS
Speaking Boldly About Yourself
"David encouraged himself in the LORD his God."[23]

- I am becoming consecrated. I am establishing something that was determined before the foundation of the world. I am being awakened spiritually to God's power and presence in my life.
- A new history is being established for me. The past is over. My relationships are better now because of my new approach. I'm not turning back.
- Eye has not seen, ear has not heard, the influence that God has prepared for me to have in the future.
- Where I have been discouraged, I will be encouraged.
- I take every city as my inheritance. I send away every spirit that is hindering souls from coming into the Kingdom of God through my influence. You are defeated. You are being pulled down. You must go under the authority of the Holy Spirit.
- Mayors, educators, businessmen, CEOs, and dope dealers will know me because of my holiness and my call. My life can be watched because I know God.

---

[23] 1 Samuel 30:6 KJV.

KINGMAKER ACTIONS
Blessed By Doing His Will
". . . a doer of the work will be blessed."[24]

God has given you absolute authority over one area of influence—yourself! It is in God's will for you to be the final authority over your emotions, words, actions and decisions. God wants you to have absolute power over them—according to His standards! God's preparation for real power, influence, and authority begins with gaining power over yourself.

When you have known sin in your life, you may be able to influence people who respond to your flesh, but you won't have the backing of God to be able to influence people on a larger scale. Get yourself right and your impact on others will follow. If you've fallen short in any of the areas mentioned in this chapter, repent. Maybe it wasn't just once or twice, but hundreds of times! Repent to God and then repent to those whom you have hurt. If you do it genuinely, you may be surprised at the weight of your words in the future!

If anyone has offended you, forgive them, build a bridge, and get over it. You can't hold unforgiveness and carry the influence that God has ordained for your life.

- List five areas where you need to influence others.
- Create a plan to influence them based on the examples of Kingmaking in this chapter and in this book.

KINGMAKER PRAYER
Submitting It All To God
". . . not my will, but thine, be done."[25]

In prayer your first priority is to cultivate a desire to hear the voice of God and a willingness to do what He says. Your goal is to become so much like God through spending time listening to Him and studying His Word that you come to the place where you know what to do without asking and you have insight into what others

---

[24] James 1:25 NKJV.
[25] Luke 22:42 KJV.

should do. In prayer you are going from glory to glory, from grace to grace. You seek God beyond your own needs. You seek Him for what He wants you to do in the lives of others. Your influence on others is godly influence, because you are consecrated.

A daddy's desire is to raise up children who can make the same decisions as their daddy would have made. It is the same with God. Ask God to show you what He is seeing, and you will be able to reach out to others and bless others as God would by giving them the truth.

You are called to be a person of influence because you know the truth, and Jesus said that the truth sets people free.[26] God does not call just a few of His people to have influence. All who know God are called to have influence. Moses led the people of Israel out of Egypt's bondage, but the whole nation was called. When you know that you are called, no matter where you are you know you have been sent there by God as an ambassador from Heaven.

Father, in Jesus' name, I praise You that at Your word the darkness in others' lives is being scattered through me. Strongholds are being broken. Thank You that You have allowed me to come to the place where I am today. Thank You that You are a champion inside of me. I have a heroes' anointing. I call for the presence of God to come into my relationships. May my mind be quickened, my senses quickened, my judgment in every way turned toward spiritual things. Let my words carry credibility and weight. May I carry a new boldness. May vision come to me specifically for my house, my children, my ministry, and the marketplace. Help me to walk with new confidence in such humility, brokenness, and contriteness that I amaze people because I am so full of wisdom and so broken. Keep me willing to go to unreasonable people. May my words never become a dripping faucet, but cause my words to carry inspiration to others. I will run to trouble because I have answers by the power and presence of God. In Jesus' name I pray. Amen.

---

[26] See John 8:32.

INDEX TO
WOMEN'S STORIES

ADDITIONAL
RESOURCES

Index to Women's Stories

More Kingmaker Resources by Wellington Boone

Kingmaker Bible Studies for Groups. Join the movement! Kingmaker groups are springing up everywhere using the book and the companion group study materials.

Kingmaker Personal Workbook . This companion to the book will help you to study, record, and meditate upon the major Kingmaker themes. You can use it for reflection and meditation in your devotional time with the Lord.

Women Who Are Kingmakers! (3-CD series). In three dynamic messages before live audiences Bishop Boone tells you how to become a woman of faith and power as you build relationships and increase your influence the Kingmaker way.

More Books by Bishop Wellington Boone

Breaking Through: Taking the Kingdom into the Culture by Out-Serving Others. The author writes, "For many Christians it would be an embarrassing moment if God called us to heaven for a spiritual evaluation." Contains profound insights into why most Americans say they believe in God yet are often unable to put that devotion into action. Historical vignettes. Themes of personal revival, conflict resolution, church unity, and racial reconciliation. (Nashville: Broadman and Holman, 1996). ISBN 0-8054-5396-2. Hardback $20.00. Paperback $10.00.

Dare to Hope: A 30-Day Journey to Hope. In Lamentations 3:21, Jeremiah was troubled but he said, "Yet I still dare to hope." Using the format of a daily journal, Bishop Boone takes the reader on a 30-day journey to hope. Each day, you read inspiring vignettes, study the Bible, pray, and document your day. Pleasing God becomes your priority. You prepare for that Great Day when you will hear God say "Well done" because you have sought His approval every day. (Atlanta: APPTE Publishing, 2009). ISBN: 978-0-9776892-8-6. Paperback $15.00.

Holy Ghost Is My Friend: A Great Friend Who Must Never Be Ignored Again, a revolutionary new way to understand our relationship with God. Jesus left behind a Comforter, the Holy Spirit, or Holy Ghost, as He is called in the King James Version of the Bible, to take His place with the disciples. Bishop Boone wrote this book to help Christians develop their Friendship with the Holy Ghost, whom Bishop Boone calls the most ignored Person of the Trinity. Commentary on the Baptism with the Holy Ghost.. 500 footnotes for personal study. Special Appendix with 272 Bible passages about the Holy Spirit. Christian Creeds defining and affirming the Deity of the Holy Spirit. (Atlanta: APPTE Publishing, 2011). ISBN-13: 9780984782109 Trade Paper. $15.00. Kindle $7.99.

Low Road To New Heights: What it Takes to Live Like Christ in the Here and Now is a proclaimed leadership guide that takes readers beyond success to significance. It teaches you how to think and act like Jesus by taking the low road of humility. It elevates those who are battered by discouragement, feel the sting of failure, and hunger for more of God. The daily practice of humility frees Christians to trust God enough to obey Him, to grow in spiritual maturity, to serve others, and to help lead others to Christ. (New York, NY: Doubleday, 2002). ISBN: 0-385-50087-4. Trade cloth. $20.00.

My Journey with God takes you toward Christ-likeness in 30 days with a foundational set of standards and daily disciplines like great Christians of the past. It gives readers a new passion for knowing God and a new pleasure in pleasing Him. God's goal for Christians is Christ-likeness. The system in Your Journey with God gives a new awareness of our need for holiness and also provides a means to get there." Inspiring stories from Christian history, personal consecration, prayer and fasting guidelines, daily journaling, scheduling, money management, and end-of-the-day accountability. (Atlanta: APPTE Publishing, coming in 2012). ISBN-13 978-0-9776892-6-2. ISBN 10: 0-9776892-6-3.Trade cloth. $25.00.

Your Wife Is Not Your Momma: How You Can Have Heaven In Your Home. Marriage is your most important preparation for the future. Includes hilarious, thought-provoking concepts for a brand new married life. Going all out for your wife, creating an environment of heaven in your home, help for the divorced to make it work the next time, insight regarding in-laws, Jesus as your First Love. Prayers, Bible quotes, challenging meditations, applications to real life. (Revised version Atlanta: APPTE Publishing, 2011). ISBN: 978-0-9776892-9-3. $15.00.

More Resources from Bishop Wellington Boone

Buga! Buga! (12-CD Series). "Buga! Buga!" means "Serious! Serious!" in Ghana, West Africa. Each message in this 12-CD series was recorded before a live audience. Over the years these key messages have inspired multitudes to change their lives.

Consecration (3-CD Series). Consecration is an often-neglected but vital aspect of Christ-likeness. The Bible says, "He who called you is holy, you also be holy in all your conduct, because it is written, 'Be holy, for I am holy' " (1 Peter 1:15-16 NKJV).

Divine Favor of God (3-CD series). Wellington Boone will build your faith to believe that God wants to flood you with His divine favor every day—just as He did when He sent His Son to save you. God has created all things richly for you to enjoy (1 Timothy 6:17 KJV).

Going All Out For Your Wife (DVD). Bishop Boone says that every man should be able to make at least one woman happy, and then he tells men how.

Heaven In Your Home (3-CD Series). Based on the book *Your Wife Is Not Your Momma*. Whether you're a woman who wants her man to change, a single or previously married person who needs new hope for marriage, or a man hoping to improve his relationship with his wife, this series is for you.

Holy Ghost Is My Friend: A Great Friend Who Must Never Be Ignored Again (Atlanta: APPTE Publishing, 2011). ISBN: 9780984782109. Trade Paper. Available on Amazon.

Husbands Going the Distance (DVD or Video). How to love your wife so much that everyone sees how much Christ must love the Church. Decide that divorce is not an option. There will be no divorce in Heaven.

Secret Place (4-CD or 2-DVD series) Jesus saw you in the crowd, and He called out to you, and you came to Him in your own secret place of prayer where you have vital communion with God through the Holy Spirit. You yield on the altar of total surrender and find that suddenly heaven is open to you.

Skandalon (3-CD series). When you meet Jesus, He offends you. He meets you at the point of your resistance and challenges your life if you are willing to be broken (Matthew 21:44) and die to your self-will.

Total Domination (16-CD set). Total Domination means taking responsibility for every area of your life. You build Christ-like relationships with individuals, communities, and nations. Ultimately, you rule and reign with Christ, because He knows He can trust you to be like Him. Four sets: Character. Christian Lifestyle, Relationships, Leadership.

Bishop Boone's resources are available online: http://www.Amazon.com
www.wellingtonboone.com   http://shop.apptepublishing.com
APPTE Publishing, 5875 Peachtree Industrial Blvd Ste 300
Norcross, GA 30092 Phone: 404-840-8443

Author Bio

"This is an incredible man of God. Every time I'm in the presence of this guy, I sense two things: This is a man who is truly a man of tremendous faith, and he's a man who is truly fearless." Bill McCartney, cofounder of Promise Keepers; former head coach, University of Colorado football team

Bishop Wellington Boone is one of today's most dynamic and sought-after Christian speakers and a trusted spiritual father to leaders who influence multitudes in North America, Africa, and around the world. He is an international ministry leader, bestselling author, featured speaker for CBN, Regent University, Focus on the Family, Promise Keepers, Campus Crusade for Christ, the Salvation Army, World Changers, and other major organizations and denominations in addition to serving his congregation, The Father's House, in Norcross, Georgia.

For many years Bishop Boone has served on the boards of major Christian ministries and produced radio and TV programs featuring his messages. Bishop Boone emphasizes Christ-like character, personal consecration, lifelong marriage, and a biblical worldview for all of life. He has founded service ministries such as the Fellowship of International Churches, Goshen Learning Centers in Africa, Global Outreach Campus Ministries, Kingmakers (women's association), and Network of Politically Active Christians in Washington, DC. He lives out his message of humility and Christ-like servanthood with Katheryn, his wife of 38 years, and three grown children.

Life Themes of Bishop Wellington Boone
♦ Celebrating Families ♦ Training Leaders ♦ Reaching the World

"Now, more than ever, the church needs servant leaders who understand the power of humility. If we truly understand these precepts and put them into practice, we will see revival. I join with Wellington Boone in his prayer that God would not let this generation pass without bringing his visitation to us."
Gordon Robertson, CEO of the Christian Broadcasting Network
Co-host of television's "The 700 Club"

Bishop Wellington Boone, "a nationally recognized pastor and speaker at Promise Keeper rallies, paints an engaging portrait of God's master plan for marriage relationships. The message is simple and, although directed at husbands, is for everyone, married couples, singles and divorcees."
Publisher's Weekly review of *Your Wife Is Not Your Momma*

"In his challenging and inspiring book *The Low Road to New Heights*, Wellington Boone identifies the source that often leads Christians to feel depressed and defeated in their lives, offering spiritual heights therapy to recover from the common curse of 'self'—pride. Humility, prayer and leading by serving remove pride."
Charisma Magazine

"This slim book is full of useful hints, designed to help readers actually follow Jesus' example of humility. . . . But this is not merely a religious how-to. Boone also threads musings on biblical stories throughout. . . . He draws on more recent historical personages, such as Harriet Tubman, in showing that humility does not make one a doormat."
Publisher's Weekly review of *Low Road to New Heights*